Your Money Shapes Your Future

A Fast-Track Guide to Financial Success

AF810074

Pachalo Mkandawire

Your Money Shapes Your Future © 2025

ISBN: 978-1-967787-47-0

The information provided in this book is designed to provide helpful information on the subjects discussed. The author's books are only meant to provide the reader with the basic knowledge of certain topics without any guarantees concerning results. This book is for educational and entertainment purposes only. While most care has been taken in compiling the information contained in this book, no responsibility can be accepted by the author for any errors or omissions that may be made. Neither can any liability be accepted by the publisher for any damages, losses, or costs resulting from using the information contained within these pages.

All trademarks and registered trademarks appearing in this book are the property of their respective owners and are used only to describe the products provided directly. Every effort has been made to properly capitalize, punctuate, identify, and attribute trademarks and register where appropriate according to industry standards.

Dedication

To my beloved parents, Zillah and Walter Mkandawire, and my dear uncle and aunt, Ted and Persis Khonje—the unwavering pillars who shaped my life.

Though my parents are no longer here, their presence remains in every lesson they taught, every sacrifice they made, and every value they instilled in me. Their love was my foundation, their wisdom my compass, and their resilience my inheritance. Zillah and Walter, you showed me that true wealth is not just in financial success but in the lives we touch, the integrity we uphold, and the legacy we leave behind. Your voices still echo in my choices, your strength still steadies me in difficult moments, and your dreams continue to fuel my own.

Uncle Ted and Aunt Persis, you have been more than family—you have been my mentors, my champions, and my guiding light. Your wisdom has been a beacon in moments of doubt, your encouragement has been a force that has propelled me forward. You have carried on the work my parents began, reinforcing the values of discipline, generosity, and perseverance. Because of you, I never walked this journey alone.

This book is not just a culmination of financial lessons—it is a tribute to all of you. Your love, your sacrifices, and your unwavering support have shaped the person I am today. And with this work, I hope to pass forward the knowledge, empowerment, and security that you so selflessly gave to me.

With deepest love and gratitude,
Pachalo

About the Author

Pachalo Mkandawire is more than just a financial expert—he is a passionate advocate for financial literacy and empowerment. With over a decade of experience in the financial industry, he has dedicated his career to simplifying the complexities of money management, investing, and wealth-building for individuals at all stages of life.

His expertise is backed by a strong academic foundation, including an MBA, a BA in Business Economics and Sociology, and a Diploma in Business Management and Business Studies. Additionally, he has completed the Financial Planning 1 and 2, Personal Financial Advice and Canadian Securities courses, further solidifying his deep understanding of financial markets, risk management, and strategic wealth planning.

But Pachalo's mission extends beyond credentials. He understands that personal finance is not just about numbers—it's about behavior, psychology, and the ability to make informed decisions that lead to long-term financial security. His book, *Your Money Shapes Your Future: A Fast-Track Guide to Financial Success*, distills years of research, industry knowledge, and real-world experience into an actionable, easy-to-follow roadmap. Whether you are a young professional navigating your first paycheck or someone looking to take control of your financial future, this book offers the essential tools to build lasting financial independence.

Through his work, Pachalo has helped countless individuals shift their mindset from financial uncertainty to financial confidence. His goal is simple: to empower readers with the knowledge and strategies they need to make smarter financial choices, eliminate unnecessary stress, and ultimately create a life of financial freedom.

Table of Contents

Introduction

In 2012, an NBA player signed a four-year, $44 million contract. By any reasonable standard, he had won the financial lottery. He was 23 years old, had never earned more than a few hundred thousand dollars a year, and now, overnight, he had more money than most people would see in a lifetime.

And yet, by 2018, he was broke.

The same story repeats itself in different forms—lottery winners who lose everything in five years, Fortune 500 executives who retire into bankruptcy, and six-figure earners who somehow live paycheck to paycheck. The numbers change, but the outcome doesn't: money, no matter how much, tends to disappear faster than expected.

The problem isn't how much people earn. It's how they manage what they earn.

Most people assume financial success is about making more money. Work hard, climb the ladder, earn bigger paychecks, and eventually, you'll be rich. That's the script we've been given. But reality tells a different story. Earning more doesn't automatically lead to financial security—just ask the high-income professionals drowning in debt. The truth is, without the right financial systems in place, making money is easy; keeping it is the hard part.

And that's exactly why this book exists.

The way we handle money has fundamentally changed. The personal finance strategies that worked a generation ago—like saving in a high-interest bank account or buying a home as a guaranteed investment—no longer deliver the same results. Today's financial world is more complex, with new tools, strategies, and pitfalls that didn't exist before.

Yet, most people are still using outdated advice.

They're told to budget every dollar, but that assumes discipline will override human psychology (it rarely does). They're told to save their way to wealth, even though inflation silently erodes their buying power. They're told that homeownership is the best investment without considering that mortgage debt, rising property taxes, and unpredictable housing markets can make it a financial trap.

In short, people are playing a new financial game with an old rulebook.

Think about your own financial situation for a moment. If you lost your job today, how long could you survive without a paycheck?

A few months? A year? Or would the next rent payment already be a problem?

Here's a reality check: nearly 64% of Americans live paycheck to paycheck, including people earning well over six figures. In Canada, it's no better—almost half of working Canadians report that they're barely covering their bills.

Most people don't fail financially because of one big mistake. It's a series of small, compounding errors: a few late credit card payments that destroy their credit score, a mortgage that seemed affordable until property taxes went up, an investment they were sure would take off but ended up crashing.

The real danger isn't financial misfortune. It's financial fragility—when even a minor setback turns into a full-blown crisis.

But it doesn't have to be that way.

There are plenty of personal finance books that preach one of two extremes.

On one side, you have the "extreme frugality" camp—the people who tell you to stop buying coffee, clip coupons, and budget every cent. The problem? No one gets rich by saving pennies.

On the other side, you have the "get-rich-quick" crowd, pushing cryptocurrency trends, high-risk investments, or the idea that passive income is a magic bullet. The problem? Most people don't need to gamble their way to wealth—they need a solid financial foundation.

This book is different.

It's built on real, practical strategies that actually work—proven methods used by people who have built and sustained wealth over time. The focus is not just on making more money but on keeping and growing it in a way that fits your life.

Instead of vague theories, this book delivers a step-by-step roadmap for financial independence. You'll learn:

- *Why budgeting doesn't work for most people (and what to do instead)*
- *How to use debt as a tool for building wealth instead of drowning in it*
- *The secret to saving more money while thinking less about it*
- *How to invest—even if you know nothing about the stock market*

- *Why most people's retirement plans are doomed and how to fix yours*
- *How to leverage financial technology to automate wealth-building*
- *The mistakes that make people lose wealth faster than they earn it—and how to avoid them*

These are not abstract concepts. Every strategy in this book is designed to be actionable.

- If you're tired of feeling like money controls you instead of the other way around—this book is for you.
- If you've ever wondered why you make good money but never seem to have enough—this book is for you.
- If you're overwhelmed by financial jargon, investing options, or conflicting advice—this book is for you.

You don't need to be a financial expert to take control of your money. You don't need a six-figure salary, a finance degree, or a stock-picking strategy. You just need a system that works—one built on understanding the new rules of money, avoiding common traps, and making small changes that lead to massive financial results.

Most people think their financial success is tied to how much they earn. But the truth is, income alone doesn't determine wealth—systems do.

Think of it like fitness. You can go to the gym and lift weights, but if your diet is terrible and you don't get enough sleep, your results will be limited. Finance works the same way. A high income won't make you rich if you don't know how to manage debt, invest wisely, or protect your assets.

A financial system is a set of habits, tools, and strategies that make financial success automatic. And that's exactly what this book will help you build.

Financial freedom isn't about luck or waiting for a higher salary. It's about understanding how money actually works—and using that knowledge to make smarter, more confident decisions.

You're about to learn how to:

- Take control of your financial future without feeling overwhelmed.
- Stop reacting to money problems and start preventing them.
- Use simple, effective strategies that create long-term wealth.

Money doesn't have to be stressful. It doesn't have to feel like a constant uphill battle. With the right knowledge and tools, you can shift from financial survival mode to financial freedom.

So, let's get started. Because your money should work for you—not the other way around.

UNDERSTANDING THE BASICS OF PERSONAL FINANCE
LIABILITIES
SAVINGS
INVESTING
MANAGEMENT
BUDGETING
ASSETS
DEBT

Chapter 1 - The $10,000 Paycheck That Left Me Broke

Nearly *60% of six-figure earners still live paycheck to paycheck.* Doctors drowning in student loans, lawyers burdened by lifestyle inflation, corporate executives who seem successful on the outside but are financially treading water. These are people who make more than enough to live comfortably—yet their bank accounts tell a different story.

Jake never thought he'd be one of them.

Jake still remembered the moment his first paycheck hit his account—$10,247.35 staring back at him from his phone screen. His hands hovered over the screen for a moment before he took a screenshot and sent it to his best friend, Mark. *Bro, we made it.*

After years of scraping by in college, stretching every dollar, and eating cheap takeout while pulling all-nighters, he had finally arrived. A real job, real money, a salary that made him feel like he was no longer just getting by—he was *winning.* He had spent years watching people struggle, listening to his parents worry about bills, overhearing conversations about layoffs and late mortgage payments. But that wasn't going to be him. He had worked too hard, landed the right job, and now he was in a position where he wouldn't have to worry about money ever again. Or at least, that's what he thought.

The first thing he did was celebrate. New apartment, new car, nights out with friends, drinks on him. He wasn't reckless—at least, not in his mind. He was rewarding himself, *enjoying* his success. Wasn't that the point? Wasn't the reason people worked so hard to be able to afford the things they wanted?

Fast forward six months and the reality of his financial decisions started to creep in like an unwelcome guest. He would wake up, check his bank account, and see a number that didn't quite make sense. Somehow, despite making more money than he had ever dreamed of, he was constantly feeling broke. His credit card balance had crept past $12,000, his car payment felt heavier every month, and the last time he checked his savings, there was barely enough to cover a decent vacation. He wasn't even sure how it had happened. *Wasn't a six-figure salary supposed to be enough?*

Jake had fallen into the trap that so many people do - believing that financial security comes from how much you earn, rather than how well you manage what you have.

Jake's situation isn't unusual. In fact, it's one of the most common financial struggles people face—especially those who suddenly start earning more. It's easy to assume that a higher paycheck solves all problems, but in reality, most financial problems don't come from not earning enough—they come from not knowing how to manage money.

Studies show that nearly 60% of people earning six figures still live paycheck to paycheck. Even doctors, lawyers, and corporate executives—people who make more than enough to live comfortably—struggle with debt, financial stress, and an overwhelming feeling that no matter how much they earn, it's never enough.

Why? Because financial security isn't about income. It's about behavior.

The mistake most people make isn't spending too much on a single splurge—it's the accumulation of small, seemingly insignificant decisions that silently drain their finances over time. The extra takeout meals, the unused subscription services, the expensive car lease to "match" a new salary. These choices don't feel like much in the moment, but over months and years, they create a financial storm that's hard to escape.

The real problem? Most people don't think about money until it's a problem.

Jake's story isn't unique—he's one of millions who assume a big paycheck guarantees financial security. But the truth is, the way you think about money shapes your financial future far more than how much you earn. Let's talk about the invisible beliefs that quietly dictate financial success—or failure.

The Stories We Tell Ourselves About Money

Most people assume their financial situation is based on how much they earn, the economy, or their circumstances. But here's something most financial experts won't tell you - your financial reality is a direct reflection of your money beliefs.

Whether you realize it or not, your subconscious thoughts about money shape every decision you make—how you spend, how you save, how you invest, and even how much you think you deserve to earn. These beliefs were planted early, shaped by your upbringing, your culture, and your past experiences. And unless you take a hard look at them, they will continue to dictate your financial future.

Some common self-limiting money beliefs that quietly sabotage financial success include -

- **"I'm just not good with money."**
- **"You have to work endlessly to be rich."**
- **"Money is stressful and complicated."**
- **"Wealthy people are greedy or dishonest."**
- **"I'll never be financially secure."**

These beliefs are not facts—but if you believe them, they become your reality. If you believe you're bad with money, you'll avoid managing it. If you believe investing is risky, you'll stay stuck in fear while others grow their wealth.

Most of us don't even realize we have financial programming running in the background. But take a moment and ask yourself -

1. **What did I learn about money growing up?**
   - Was money always scarce, or was it abundant?
   - Were your parents savers or spenders?
   - Did they view money as a source of stress or a tool for freedom?
2. **What messages have I internalized about wealth?**
   - Do I believe making money requires suffering and endless hard work?
   - Do I secretly feel guilty about wanting more financial security?
   - Do I associate financial success with greed or corruption?
3. **How do these beliefs affect my financial choices?**
   - Do I avoid looking at my bank statements because I feel anxious?

- Do I feel like "there's never enough," even when I make more?
- Do I sabotage myself by spending impulsively or delaying savings?

Once you identify the beliefs that hold you back, you can rewrite them.

Instead of - **"I'm bad with money."** → Reframe it as - **"I'm learning to manage money wisely."**
Instead of - **"Wealthy people are greedy."** → Reframe it as - **"Money allows me to create opportunities for myself and others."**
Instead of - **"I'll never be rich."** → Reframe it as - **"I am building financial security one smart decision at a time."**

These small mental shifts are powerful because your brain follows the beliefs you reinforce. When you change the way you think about money, you naturally start making different choices—ones that bring you closer to financial freedom instead of keeping you stuck.

Money is not just a practical tool—it's a psychological game. And if you don't address the invisible beliefs running your financial life, no budget, investment plan, or debt strategy will stick. This is why two people with the same income can have completely different financial outcomes. One sees money as an opportunity, the other as a constant struggle. One makes confident decisions, the other is paralyzed by fear.

Your beliefs are not set in stone.

If you shift from a scarcity mindset ("There's never enough") to an abundance mindset ("There are always ways to grow financially"), your actions will follow. If you stop seeing money as the enemy and start seeing it as a tool, you'll use it wisely instead of fearing it.

The Four Pillars of Financial Success

To build true financial security—one where you don't wake up anxious about bills, where unexpected expenses don't send you into panic mode, where money feels like a tool rather than a source of stress—you need to understand the four key areas of personal finance. These four pillars separate those who control their money from those who feel controlled by it.

1. Budgeting - Knowing Where Your Money Goes

Most people resist budgeting because they think it's about restricting what they can do. They picture spreadsheets, endless tracking, and the joy being sucked out of their spending. But budgeting isn't about restriction—it's about control.

If you don't know where your money is going, it's impossible to build wealth. A budget isn't about *spending less*—it's about spending intentionally. It's the difference between wondering where your paycheck went and knowing exactly how much you can afford to save, invest, and spend on things you enjoy.

Jake never tracked his spending. He assumed that as long as his paycheck covered his bills and credit card payments, he was doing fine. But fine wasn't good enough. Every month, small amounts of untracked spending—$20 here, $50 there—added up, and soon, he was spending more than he realized.

Budgeting doesn't mean cutting out fun. It means designing a system where you spend money on the things that matter and cut out the waste.

2. Saving - Protecting Yourself from Life's Curveballs

One of the biggest financial myths people believe is that saving is only possible when you earn more. In reality, most people don't save because they don't make it a priority—not because they don't have enough.

Think about it - if you got a $500 emergency expense right now, could you cover it without stress? Nearly 60% of Americans can't. Why? Because most people only save whatever's left after they spend—when the reality is you should save first, then spend what's left.

Jake's bank account was a revolving door—money came in, money went out. No cushion, no safety net. If he had started saving just 10% of his income when he first got his job, he would have had $6,000 saved within six months—without changing his lifestyle.

3. Debt - The Silent Wealth Killer

Not all debt is bad—but most people have the kind that keeps them stuck.

Jake thought making minimum payments on his credit cards was enough. He didn't realize that his $12,000 balance was costing him nearly $2,500 a year in interest alone. By only making minimum payments, he was on track to be in debt for over a decade.

This is the trap of high-interest debt - it keeps you working for banks instead of for yourself. Credit cards, car loans, and personal loans make it easy to spend money you don't have—but the cost of borrowing is what keeps people stuck in the cycle of paycheck-to-paycheck living.

4. The Power of Investing (Even If You Start Small)

One of the biggest misconceptions about investing is that you need a lot of money to get started. This is one of the most damaging myths that keeps people from building wealth early in life.

In reality, investing works best when you start with small amounts over a long period of time. It's not about throwing huge sums into the stock market overnight—it's about consistently putting money into investments and letting time do the heavy lifting.

Let's say you start investing just $100 a month at age 25. That's about $3.30 a day—less than a cup of coffee. If you put that money into a basic index fund that earns an average of 8% per year, here's what happens -

- By age 35, you'll have around $18,000.
- By age 45, it grows to $60,000.
- By age 55, it's over $150,000.
- And by the time you retire at 65, that tiny $100-a-month habit has turned into $375,000+.

Now, imagine if you had waited. If you started at 35 instead of 25, your total would be less than half of that—even if you saved the exact same amount every month.

This is the power of compound growth. The longer your money is invested, the more time it has to grow exponentially. Wealthy people don't invest because they're rich—they're rich because they invest.

Jake's biggest realization wasn't just that he had been bad with money—it was that he had never actually *learned* how to be good with it. Nobody had ever taught him how to manage his paycheck, how to build wealth, or how to avoid the mistakes that quietly drained his financial future. His school had spent years teaching him calculus and literary analysis, but not once had a teacher explained how credit card interest worked or why investing early mattered. And his parents? They had done their best, but they had always struggled with money, too. They told him to "save," but what did that even mean? Save for what? How much? Where?

This is the reality for most people. We are left to figure out money on our own, often after we've already made mistakes. The irony is that financial literacy is one of the most valuable skills a person can have, yet almost no one is taught how to use it. People assume that financial success is about intelligence or background, but it isn't—it's about understanding a few key principles and applying them consistently.

How Wealth is Actually Built (And Why Most People Get It Wrong)

Most people assume the rich get richer simply because they have more money to begin with. But that's only half the story. The real reason they get richer is because they use money differently than everyone else.

Suppose you compare two people earning the exact same salary. In that case, their financial outcomes can be dramatically different—not because one is luckier, but because one understands how money works, and the other doesn't.

Let's break this down with a simple example -

- **Person** A spends most of their paycheck on day-to-day expenses, keeps whatever is left in a checking account, and occasionally treats themselves because, hey, they work hard. They don't think about investing because it feels complicated, and they assume they'll "figure it out later."
- **Person B** lives the same lifestyle but makes two small adjustments - They automatically invest 15% of their income before spending anything else, and they avoid high-interest debt.

At first, the difference between these two people is invisible. In the first year, both of them are making roughly the same financial decisions. But fast forward ten years, and the gap between them is massive -

- **Person A** still feels like they're just scraping by. Their savings are minimal, they're carrying some debt, and they're starting to feel anxious about the future.
- **Person B** has quietly built a six-figure investment portfolio, earns passive income from their money, and has financial flexibility that Person A can't even see.

This isn't a matter of luck. It's a matter of understanding how money grows over time. And the key difference is one thing - Person B started early, while Person A kept putting it off.

The Fastest Way to Improve Your Financial Future (Starting Today)

Most people assume that fixing their finances will take years. And while building wealth does take time, changing your financial trajectory can happen almost instantly.

Here's how to dramatically change your financial future starting today -

1. Automate Savings & Investments – Set up an automatic transfer to a separate account every time you get paid. Start small if needed, but be consistent.
2. Eliminate High-Interest Debt First – Credit cards with high interest are financial quicksand. Pay them off aggressively.
3. Start Investing Now – Even if it's just $50 a month, get started. The habit is more important than the amount.
4. Live Below Your Means (But Enjoy Life Too) – The goal isn't deprivation—it's intentional spending. Cut wasteful expenses, but keep what brings you real joy.

These changes don't require a huge salary. They don't require financial expertise. They just require consistency.

Jake finally understood what had been missing all along. It wasn't about making more money—it was about knowing what to do with the money he already had. For years, he had assumed that wealth was something that happened to *other* people—people who had better jobs, higher salaries, or family money. But now, he realized something that changed everything - Wealth isn't about how much you make. It's about what you do with what you make.

Think about it - schools drill students on algebra, Shakespeare, and the periodic table, yet almost no one leaves high school knowing how to file taxes, manage debt, or build wealth. This massive education gap means most people stumble into adulthood, completely unprepared for the financial decisions that will shape the rest of their lives.

The consequences of this gap are brutal. Without financial literacy, people are left to figure things out the hard way—through costly mistakes.

- They sign up for credit cards without understanding how compound interest works against them.
- They lease expensive cars without realizing they are paying for something they will never own.
- They wait too long to start investing, believing it's something they can "get to later."

The cost of not knowing is staggering. And the worst part? Financial ignorance doesn't just impact money—it impacts everything. It dictates career choices, the ability to buy a home, stress levels, relationships, and even health.

In the next chapter, we'll dive into how to set financial goals that actually work—without the common mistakes that keep most people stuck.

ESTABLISHING FINANCIAL GOALS SHORT, MEDIUM & LONG TERM

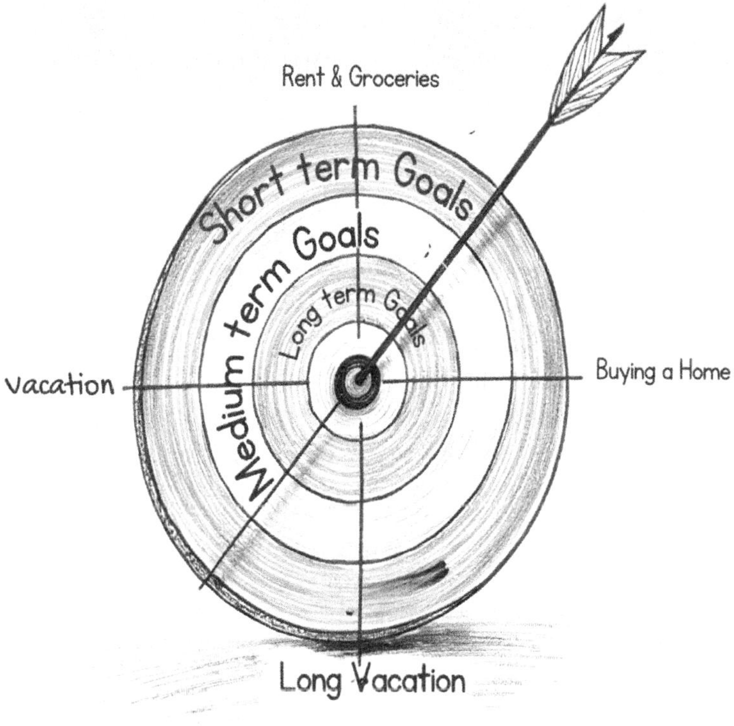

Chapter 2 - How to Stop Winging It with Money

On September 15, 2008, Lehman Brothers collapsed, triggering the worst financial crisis since the Great Depression. Within weeks, millions of people lost their jobs, homes, and retirement savings. But while some families were forced into bankruptcy, others rode out the storm relatively unscathed.

It wasn't income. Some six-figure earners were wiped out while middle-class families stayed afloat. It wasn't luck either—many "lucky" people had actually been preparing for years without even realizing it.

The real difference? They had financial goals.

The families who weathered the crisis weren't necessarily richer, but they had emergency funds, manageable debt, and long-term investments that could recover. Meanwhile, those who had no financial plan were left scrambling, realizing too late that living paycheck to paycheck is a dangerous gamble.

The harsh truth? Most people don't plan their finances—they react to them. Bills come, money goes. A new expense pops up, and they adjust on the fly. They believe they'll "figure it out later." But later always comes—sometimes in the form of a recession, a job loss, or an emergency that doesn't wait for them to catch up.

That's why this chapter isn't just about *setting goals*. It's about creating a financial system that protects you from life's uncertainties. Because here's the truth - You don't rise to the level of your income. You fall to the level of your financial plan.

Most people set financial goals the wrong way, which is why they rarely achieve them. They have good intentions but lack the structure needed to succeed.

Here's what usually happens -

Problem #1 - Their Goals Are Too Vague

When people say, **"I want to save more,"** what does that actually mean? $100 a month? $10,000 this year? Without a specific number and timeline, there's no real direction. It's like saying, *"I want to get in shape"* but never deciding what that looks like—losing 10 pounds? Running a marathon? Without clarity, the goal is just a vague hope.

Problem #2 - They Focus on the Goal, Not the Process

Setting a goal is easy. But **most people don't plan how they'll achieve it.**

Take two people who want to buy a house -

- **Person A** - Says, *"I'll buy a house in five years"* but never calculates how much they'll need for a down payment or how much they should be saving each month.
- **Person B** - Sets a monthly savings target, opens a high-yield savings account, and cuts unnecessary expenses to make it happen.

Guess who's actually buying a house in five years?

Problem #3 - They Don't Review or Adjust Their Goals

Financial goals **aren't set in stone.** Life changes—your job, your expenses, your priorities. But most people **set a goal once and forget about it**, which is why they fail.

- A single person saving aggressively for a house might need to **adjust** when they get married.
- A young professional might need to **shift** their investing strategy after a promotion.
- A new parent might have to **reprioritize** emergency savings over early retirement planning.

Most financial failures aren't due to lack of income. They're due to lack of a **clear plan.** But when you fix these three mistakes, you shift from *reacting* to money to *controlling* it.

The Right Way to Set Short-, Medium-, and Long-Term Goals

In 1980, a young professor named Terry Odean sat in his university office, staring at a strange pattern emerging from his research. He had been analyzing the investment behavior of individual stock traders, and one thing was clear—most of them were making decisions that seemed entirely irrational. They chased hot stocks, panicked at market dips, and ignored slow, steady gains in favor of risky bets. It wasn't that they lacked intelligence. The problem was **they had no framework for making financial decisions**.

Odean's research would later contribute to the field of behavioral finance, proving what many of us already suspected - **left to our own devices, humans are terrible at managing money.** Not because we don't try but because we rely too much on impulse and too little on structured planning. This is why most people drift financially—they don't set goals the right way. They think in vague terms - *"I need to save more." "I want to be better with money."* But without breaking goals into clear categories, most financial plans collapse under the weight of daily life.

Short-Term Goals - The Immediate Future (0–2 Years)

Short-term goals are about building financial stability right now. They're the foundation of everything else. If long-term goals are skyscrapers, short-term goals are the concrete and steel reinforcements that keep them from toppling over. The biggest mistake people make is assuming they can focus only on long-term goals like retirement while ignoring the financial problems directly in front of them. But the first rule of wealth-building isn't investing—it's making sure you're not one emergency away from financial disaster.

Consider this - A survey by the Federal Reserve found that nearly 40% of Americans couldn't cover a $400 emergency expense without borrowing money. That means nearly half the population is walking a financial tightrope, hoping they don't slip. The first short-term goal, then, is simple but critical - build an emergency fund. This is not an investment—it's protection. Without a buffer of at least three to six months' worth of expenses, even the best financial plans can be wiped out by a single unexpected event—a medical bill, a job loss, or a broken-down car.

The second short-term goal is eliminating high-interest debt. Many people don't realize this, but carrying a credit card balance month to month is one of the fastest ways to destroy wealth. The average credit card interest rate hovers around 20%, meaning that if you owe $10,000 on a card and only make minimum payments, you could be paying that debt off for over a decade, spending thousands in interest. It doesn't matter if you're investing in stocks or have a well-diversified portfolio—if you're losing 20% a year to credit card interest, you're financially bleeding out.

Short-term goals are about getting your financial house in order. They don't generate wealth, but they ensure you don't lose it before you even have a chance to build.

Medium-Term Goals - The Transition Stage (2–10 Years)

If short-term goals are about survival, medium-term goals are about stability and progress. This is where real financial transformation begins because these goals bridge the gap between "getting by" and actually building something meaningful.

Take homeownership, for example. Many financial experts argue whether buying a home is a good investment, but the data suggests one thing clearly - people who own homes tend to accumulate more wealth over time than those who don't. Not necessarily because homes appreciate at a rapid pace, but because homeownership forces disciplined saving.

Here's why - A renter might spend $1,500 a month on rent for 30 years with nothing to show for it at the end. A homeowner, on the other hand, makes a similar payment on a mortgage, slowly building equity. Even if the home doesn't appreciate significantly, after 30 years they own a valuable asset outright. This is why homeownership—when done wisely—is one of the most effective medium-term financial goals.

But not all medium-term goals are about real estate. Investing aggressively in retirement accounts is another key milestone. This is where most people get tripped up. They think they have plenty of time to start investing for retirement, but the math tells a different story.

Consider two people;

- Person A starts investing at 25, putting away $500 a month until age 35, then stops contributing.
- Person B waits until 35 to start investing and contributes $500 a month until they retire at 65.

Who ends up with more money? Person A.

Even though they only invested for ten years, their money had a 30-year head start, compounding and growing exponentially. Person B, despite investing for three times as long, ends up with significantly less. This is the power of time in investing.

This is why medium-term financial goals matter - They create opportunities that aren't immediately obvious. While short-term goals prevent financial disasters, medium-term goals open doors to financial independence.

Long-Term Goals - The Endgame (10+ Years)

If short-term goals are about survival and medium-term goals are about growth, long-term goals are about freedom. The difference between the financially secure and the financially struggling isn't just how much they make—it's how early they start preparing for the future.

Think about this - Every dollar you invest in your 20s has the potential to grow by a factor of 30 by the time you retire. Every dollar you invest in your 40s might only triple in that same time frame. The longer you wait to focus on long-term financial security, the harder you have to work to catch up.

For most people, the ultimate long-term goal is retirement. But "retirement" is a vague term. What does that actually mean? How much money do you need? The answer depends on your financial independence number—the amount of money you need invested to live comfortably without working.

A common rule of thumb is the 4% rule, which states that you can safely withdraw 4% of your investment portfolio annually without running out of money. If you need $50,000 a year to live, that means you need a nest egg of about $1.25 million to retire comfortably.

This number shocks many people, but it shouldn't. It's not about winning the lottery or making risky investments—it's about starting early and being consistent.

But here's the biggest long-term financial mistake - thinking you can't start yet. People assume they need to have extra money to invest, but the reality is, you should be investing while still working on your short- and medium-term goals. Waiting for the "right time" is the surest way to never start at all.

Long-term goals aren't about what you'll do "someday." They are about the small, consistent steps you take today that will determine whether you have financial freedom—or financial regret—in the future.

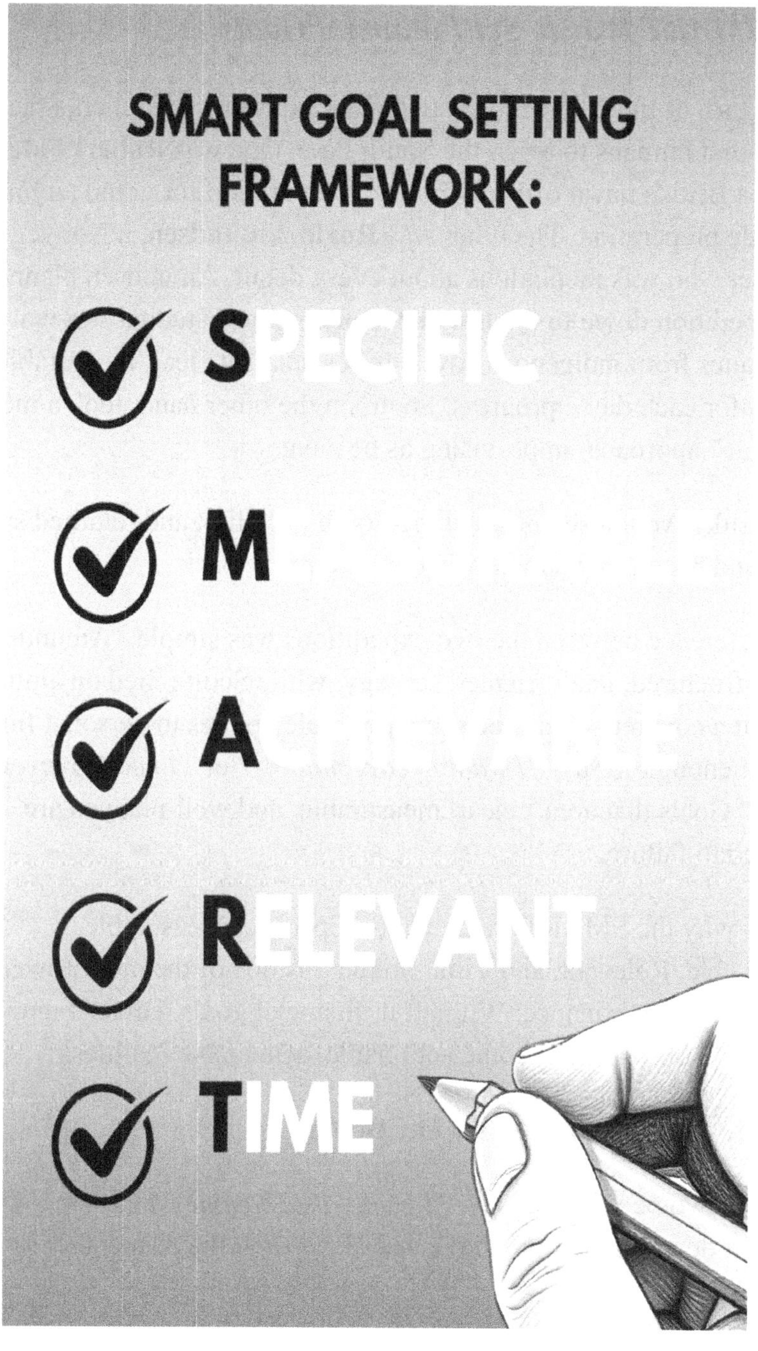
SMART GOAL SETTING FRAMEWORK:
SPECIFIC
M
A
RELEVANT
TIME

The SMART Way to Set Financial Goals

At the turn of the 20th century, two rival explorers set out on a race to be the first humans to reach the South Pole. One was **Robert Falcon Scott**, a British naval officer who had a reputation for grand ambition but little preparation. The other was **Roald Amundsen**, a Norwegian explorer who was meticulous about every detail. Amundsen planned his expedition down to the last ounce of supplies, studied survival techniques from indigenous Arctic tribes, and set clear, measurable targets for each day's progress. Scott, on the other hand, took a more "flexible" approach, improvising as he went.

The result? Amundsen reached the South Pole first and returned safely. Scott and his entire team perished on their way back.

The difference between the two expeditions was simple - Amundsen had a structured, goal-oriented strategy, while Scott relied on ambition without a concrete plan. The same principle applies to personal finance. It's not enough to say, *"I want to save money,"* or *"I need to invest more."* Goals that aren't clear, measurable, and well-planned are doomed to failure.

This is why the SMART framework—Specific, Measurable, Achievable, Relevant, and Time-bound—is one of the most powerful tools in personal finance. Without it, financial goals remain vague dreams. With it, they become actionable, achievable realities.

Specific - The More Precise, The Better

Imagine two people both say, *"I want to save money this year."* One writes it down in their notebook and leaves it at that. The other says, *"I* *will save $5,000 by December 31st by setting aside $416 each month."* Who is more likely to succeed?

Vague financial goals are like throwing darts in the dark—you might hit something, but it won't be what you were aiming for. **A goal needs to be laser-focused.** Instead of saying, *"I want to save for retirement,"* say, *"I will contribute $500 per month to my TFSA and max out my RRSP contributions."* Instead of *"I want to buy a house someday,"* say, *"I will save $20,000 for a down payment within three years by cutting non-essential spending by 20%."*

Measurable - Track It Like a Scientist

In 1961, President John F. Kennedy stood before Congress and announced that the United States would land a man on the moon before the decade was over. That goal wasn't just ambitious—it was measurable. It had a clear outcome - either an astronaut would walk on the moon, or he wouldn't.

This is exactly how financial goals should work. If you can't measure your progress, you'll never know if you're on track. Want to get out of debt? Track how much you're paying off each month. Want to build an emergency fund? Set a target and monitor your balance. Want to retire early? Calculate your FI (financial independence) number and track your investments.

Numbers bring accountability. If you say, *"I want to invest more,"* there's no way to gauge success. But if you say, *"I will increase my portfolio by $50,000 in five years by investing $833 per month,"* then every month, you can check if you're hitting the target. And if you're not? You adjust.

Achievable - Dream Big, But Stay Realistic

There's a fine line between an inspiring goal and an impossible one. Telling yourself you'll save $100,000 in a year when you make $50,000 is setting yourself up for failure. The key to goal setting is finding the balance between ambition and reality.

This doesn't mean aiming low. It means building a staircase rather than a leap of faith. If your goal is to become financially independent, break it into smaller, achievable steps. Maybe the first step is eliminating $10,000 of debt. The next is maxing out your retirement accounts. Then, saving enough to cover a year's worth of expenses. When goals are achievable, they generate momentum. And momentum is what keeps you going when motivation fades.

Relevant - Your Money, Your Life

There's no point in setting goals that don't align with what you actually care about. Some people obsess over early retirement. Others want financial security while enjoying their present. Some dream of homeownership, while others prioritize travel. Think about why you want to reach a certain financial milestone. If you're saving aggressively but have no clear purpose, it's easy to lose motivation. But if your goal is tied to something personally meaningful—like providing a stable future for your family or achieving the freedom to leave a job you hate—then it becomes much more powerful.

Ask yourself - Why does this goal matter? What will it allow me to do? The clearer the personal connection, the stronger your commitment will be.

Time-Bound - Without a Deadline, It's Just a Wish

A goal without a deadline is just a vague intention. Deadlines create urgency. They push you to act now rather than *"someday."*

Imagine two people both want to pay off $20,000 in student loans. One says, *"I'll pay it off as soon as I can."* The other says, *"I will pay off $20,000 in two years by making $833 monthly payments."* Who do you think will actually follow through?

Deadlines force action. **They create pressure, and pressure fuels discipline.** They also allow for course correction—if you fall behind, you can adjust instead of drifting aimlessly.

Now, let's put it all together. Instead of setting vague goals like -

"I need to start saving."
"I should invest more."
"I want to be better with money."

Use the SMART framework -

"I will save $10,000 in the next 12 months by cutting discretionary spending and increasing my income through freelance work."
"I will pay off my $5,000 credit card debt within a year by making $420 monthly payments."
"I will contribute $500 per month to my TFSA and increase my contributions by 5% annually."

The difference is night and day. One is vague, the other is a clear, structured plan. The more precise your financial goals are, the more likely you are to reach them.

Building a Financial Roadmap - From Goals to Action

Setting goals is easy. Sticking to them is the hard part.

It's why millions of people make New Year's resolutions—then abandon them by February. The gym memberships go unused. The reading lists remain untouched. The savings plans fall apart after the first unexpected expense. The problem isn't motivation. It's structure.

Financial success isn't about willpower. **It's about having a system.** The people who consistently save, invest, and build wealth don't do it because they have more discipline than you. They do it because they've set up a framework that makes success inevitable.

This is why **a financial roadmap**—a clear, structured plan that guides your money decisions—is essential. It's the difference between drifting through life, hoping you'll "figure it out," and having a strategy that keeps you moving forward, no matter what life throws at you.

Let's break down how to build one.

Step 1 - Assess Where You Are Right Now

Before you plan a road trip, you need to know your starting point.

Most people avoid this step because they're afraid of what they'll find. They don't want to see the reality of their finances—the credit card debt, the paycheck-to-paycheck cycle, the savings account that never seems to grow. But ignoring your financial situation doesn't make it better. It makes it worse.

The first step in building a roadmap is taking a brutally honest look at your money -

- **Income -** How much do you actually bring in after taxes?
- **Expenses -** Where is your money going every month?
- **Debt -** What do you owe, and what are the interest rates?
- **Savings & Investments -** How much do you have set aside for emergencies, retirement, and future goals?

Write it all down. No judgment, no excuses—just facts. **This is your financial baseline.**

Step 2 - Create a Money System That Works Automatically

Most people try to "manage" their money by sheer effort. They track every purchase manually, remind themselves to save, and hope they'll remember to pay their bills on time. But, effort-based systems fail because willpower is limited.

The key is automation.

- **Pay Yourself First -** The moment you get paid, set up automatic transfers to savings and investments before you spend a dime.
- **Set Up Separate Accounts for Each Goal -** Emergency fund, travel fund, down payment fund—keep them separate so you don't "accidentally" spend your future on takeout.
- **Automate Debt Payments -** If you're paying off debt, set up automatic payments that exceed the minimums. This prevents the temptation to "skip" a month.

Step 3 - Adjust for the Unexpected (Because It's Coming)

The biggest mistake people make when creating financial plans? They assume nothing will go wrong. But life isn't predictable. Cars break down. Medical bills pop up. The economy shifts. The difference between people who stay on track and those who fall apart is preparation. You need financial shock absorbers.

- **Emergency Fund First -** If you don't have at least 3–6 months' worth of expenses saved, that's priority #1. No investment, no big purchases—just build a financial safety net.
- **Plan for the Unpredictable -** Set aside a "life happens" fund for unexpected but inevitable expenses—car repairs, home maintenance, surprise medical bills.
- **Use Percent-Based Budgeting -** Instead of rigidly allocating fixed amounts, work with percentages. That way, if your income fluctuates, your savings and investing adjust automatically.

Step 4 - Review, Adjust, and Stay Flexible

A financial plan isn't something you create once and forget. **It's a living, breathing document that evolves with your life.**

Set checkpoints -

- **Monthly -** Quick budget check—did you overspend? Where can you adjust?
- **Quarterly -** Investment and debt review—are you making progress? Do you need to rebalance?
- **Annually -** Big-picture assessment—have your goals changed? Do you need to shift priorities?

Flexibility is key. Your goals will change. Maybe you'll decide homeownership isn't worth it. Maybe you'll realize early retirement is more achievable than you thought. Maybe you'll want to work less and travel more.

If you take nothing else from this chapter, take this;

Wealth isn't built on big, dramatic moves. It's built on boring, consistent habits.

The people who become financially successful aren't the ones who try to time the stock market, chase crypto trends, or bet big on the next get-rich-quick scheme. They're the ones who set goals, automate their finances, and stick to their plan for years. And over time, these simple habits compound into life-changing results.

If you set clear financial goals, create a system that makes success inevitable, and stay flexible enough to adjust along the way—you will build wealth. Not overnight. Not in a straight line. But steadily, surely, and permanently.

The question isn't whether you can do it. The question is whether you're willing to stick with it long enough for the results to show.

The next chapter will show you exactly how to take the first steps—starting now.

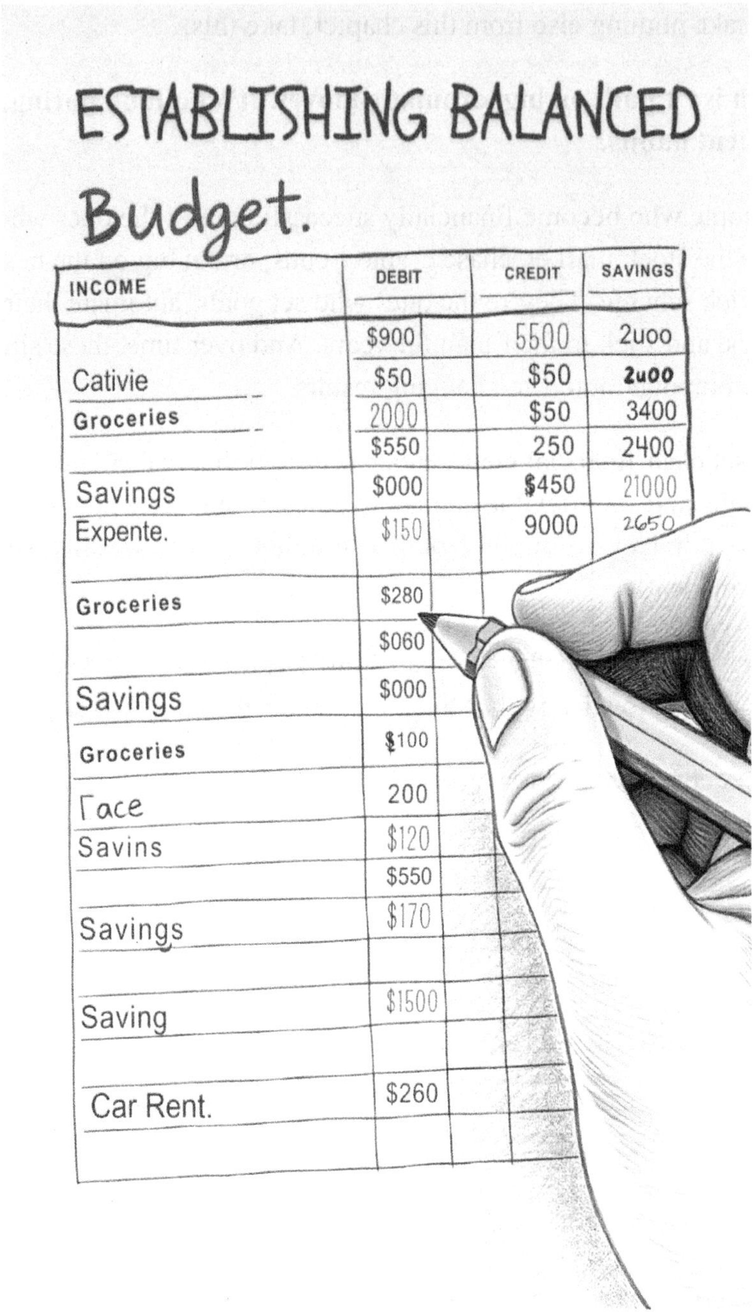
ESTABLISHING BALANCED
Budget.
INCOME
DEBIT
CREDIT
SAVINGS
$900
5500
2uoo
Cativie
$50
$50
2uoo
Groceries
2000
$50
3400
$550
250
2400
Savings
$000
$450
21000
Expente.
$150
9000
2650
Groceries
$280
$060
Savings
$000
Groceries
$100
Face
200
Savins
$120
$550
Savings
$170
Saving
$1500
Car Rent.
$260

Chapter 3 - The Budgeting Myth—Why Conventional Wisdom Fails

A bright young analyst named Tom began his career at a Wall Street investment firm. He had spent his college years studying spreadsheets, cash flow models, and risk assessments. He knew the difference between good debt and bad debt. He understood compound interest. He could spot a mispriced stock in seconds. Yet, despite his financial expertise, Tom had a personal problem - he could not stick to a budget.

Every January, he'd sit down with a crisp new notebook, a financial calculator, and a sense of determination. He meticulously planned out his spending categories—groceries, rent, dining out, travel, entertainment. He built a detailed system to track every dollar. And yet, by March, the budget would inevitably crumble.

A surprise expense—an emergency flight home, a car repair, a forgotten subscription renewal—would throw his projections off course. Then came the slow unraveling. The careful logging of purchases in a spreadsheet turned into occasional notes scribbled in the margins of a planner. By summer, the entire exercise was abandoned. Tom wasn't alone—his colleagues, many of whom managed millions of dollars for institutional clients, had the same problem.

The irony was obvious. Here were some of the most financially savvy people in the country—people whose jobs revolved around allocating capital efficiently—and they couldn't manage their own money effectively.

Why?

Because budgeting, at least in the way we've been taught, doesn't work. Not in the way we think it should.

Tom's story is hardly unique. Every year, millions of people set up budgets with the best of intentions, only to abandon them within months. The pattern repeats itself across all income levels - whether you earn $40,000 a year or $400,000, the challenge remains the same.

The common belief is that budgeting fails because people lack discipline. If only they were more responsible, more organized, more committed to tracking their spending, they would finally get their finances in order.

But this assumption is deeply flawed. Budgeting doesn't fail because people are bad with money. It fails because traditional budgeting is built on unrealistic expectations of human behavior.

The Willpower Fallacy

People assume that budgeting is a matter of willpower—that if you just track your expenses carefully enough, you'll be able to control your spending. But willpower is a finite resource. Studies in behavioral psychology have shown that the more decisions we make in a day, the harder it becomes to exert self-control.

Think of it this way - at the start of the day, when your energy is high, you might have no problem sticking to your plan. You resist the temptation to buy an overpriced latte. You walk past the bakery without a second glance. You decline the unnecessary Amazon purchase.

But as the day goes on, your willpower wears down. You've made a hundred small decisions—what to wear, what to eat, how to respond to emails, whether to hit the gym—and by the time dinner rolls around, your brain is exhausted. That's when you cave. That's when you order takeout instead of cooking. That's when you justify the $200 impulse buy.

This isn't just a personal weakness—it's how our brains work.

Willpower alone cannot sustain a budget. A system built on constant decision-making is destined to fail.

The Spreadsheet Trap

Most people approach budgeting the way they were taught in school - by **making a spreadsheet**. The logic seems sound—if you list your income, track your expenses, and set limits for each category, you should be able to manage your money effortlessly.

Except that's not how people actually spend money.

Spreadsheets are inherently backward-looking. They tell you what happened last month, last week, yesterday. But they don't help you **make real-time decisions**. You don't consult your Excel file when standing in a checkout line. You don't pull out your budget before making a spontaneous dinner reservation. **By the time you review your spending, the money is already gone.**

More importantly, traditional budgeting assumes that life is **predictable**—that each month looks roughly the same. But anyone who has ever had **a car break down, a medical bill appear, or a friend's wedding pop up out of nowhere** knows that's not how real life works.

This is why budgeting often feels like a game of guilt and failure. You set limits, break them, and then feel like you've failed. The problem isn't you—it's the budgeting method itself.

The Illusion of Predictability

The single biggest flaw in traditional budgeting is the assumption that **expenses follow a predictable pattern**. In reality, spending is lumpy, irregular, and often **driven by emotions** rather than logic.

If you look at your annual spending, you'll notice something strange - very little of it is truly consistent. Sure, rent or mortgage payments remain the same, but everything else fluctuates. Some months, you might spend very little on eating out, and then a friend visits from out of town, and suddenly you're at restaurants three nights a week. Some months, you might be frugal, and then an emotional event—stress, celebration, boredom—leads to an unexpected shopping spree.

Why "Tracking Every Dollar" Doesn't Work—And What Does

There is something uniquely frustrating about doing everything "right" and still feeling like you're failing. For years, conventional financial wisdom has pushed the idea that tracking every dollar—every morning coffee, every grocery receipt, every Uber ride—is the key to financial control. If you know where your money is going, the logic goes: you can make better financial decisions, cut unnecessary expenses, and build wealth. But in reality, most people who try this approach don't become better at managing their money—they just become better at feeling guilty about it.

In 2018, Daniel, a software engineer in Austin, Texas, decided he was going to take control of his finances in the most meticulous way possible. His goal was simple - optimize his spending to save as much as possible. He built a color-coded spreadsheet, linked it to his bank accounts, and began tracking every single expense. Every $4.75 latte. Every $12.89 Uber ride. Every impulse Amazon purchase. At first, it felt empowering. Seeing every transaction laid out like a digital autopsy gave him a sense of control. For the first time, he could see where his money was actually going.

But a few months in, something changed. The tracking started to feel less like a tool and more like a burden. He found himself hesitating before making even the smallest purchases, calculating whether he could justify them in his meticulously planned budget. If he went over in one category, he felt like he had failed, even if his savings goals were still intact. He spent more time adjusting numbers than actually enjoying the benefits of his hard work. What started as a strategy for financial freedom had turned into an exhausting game of self-surveillance.

Daniel's story is not unique. In fact, it illustrates a fundamental problem with the way traditional budgeting is taught. Tracking every dollar doesn't create better financial habits—it creates financial anxiety. Instead of helping people make smarter money decisions, it turns every spending choice into a moral dilemma. And worst of all, it shifts focus away from what actually makes people wealthy - **big financial decisions, not small spending habits.**

The reason tracking every dollar doesn't work is simple - it makes budgeting feel like a punishment. When people start a budget, they do so with the best of intentions. They want to be more responsible, they want to save more, they want to feel in control. But the moment they start micromanaging their finances down to the penny, they begin treating money as something to be rationed rather than something to be managed. Every discretionary purchase, no matter how small, feels like a betrayal of their long-term financial goals. The result? Burnout, frustration, and eventually, abandonment of the entire system.

There's also the sheer impracticality of it. Keeping up with every transaction takes time, and time is a limited resource. Most people don't abandon budgeting because they don't care about their money—they abandon it because it becomes **too much work**. Manually logging expenses, categorizing purchases, and adjusting budgets every time something unexpected happens is mentally exhausting. And for what? So you can know exactly how much you spent on gas last month? That's not financial control—that's bookkeeping.

Then there's the problem of **false precision**. Let's say you carefully budget $500 a month for groceries. One month, you come in at $480, and the next month, you hit $515. Are you failing? No, but when budgets are too rigid, they make natural fluctuations feel like violations of the system. This kind of thinking is what leads people to give up entirely when they "go over budget" in one category, even if they're still financially on track overall. Money doesn't work in perfect, predictable patterns, and any budgeting system that assumes it does is doomed to fail.

What Actually Works - Systems Over Spreadsheets

So, if tracking every dollar doesn't work, what does? The answer isn't more discipline or better tracking apps—it's designing a system where good financial decisions happen automatically. Wealthy people don't track every dollar. They don't spend their evenings reconciling budgets or agonizing over whether they went $20 over in their dining-out category. Instead, they set up systems that ensure their biggest financial goals happen first—and then they let the rest take care of itself.

The best way to do this is to automate financial priorities before spending even begins. This means setting up automatic transfers so that a percentage of your income immediately goes into savings, investments, and debt repayment before you have a chance to spend it. If your financial priorities are handled first, you don't need to track every dollar—you only need to ensure you're not spending more than what's left.

This system works because it removes the need for willpower. If your savings are automated, you don't have to remember to transfer money into an investment account or worry about whether you'll have enough left at the end of the month. The decision has already been made for you. And unlike tracking every dollar, which requires constant effort, automation requires almost no ongoing work.

Another key to effective budgeting is focusing on big financial wins instead of small spending habits. Conventional budgeting wisdom obsesses over cutting out lattes and restaurant meals, but the reality is that small expenses aren't what keep most people from building wealth—big financial decisions are. Where you live, what car you drive, how much debt you take on—these are the choices that determine long-term financial success. Someone who spends $4,000 a year on rent instead of $6,000 will accumulate more savings than someone who cuts out lattes for a decade.

This is why financially successful people focus on optimizing the big stuff and letting the small expenses work themselves out. They negotiate salaries, they reduce fixed costs, they avoid unnecessary debt. They don't track every dollar because they don't need to—their financial system ensures that they save and invest automatically, so whatever they spend after that is irrelevant.

How to Implement a No-Tracking Budget That Actually Works

For those who still want some structure, the best alternative to tracking every dollar is a cash-flow-based budgeting system. Instead of dividing spending into dozens of detailed categories, you divide it into three broad sections -

1. **Fixed Costs -** Rent, insurance, utilities—expenses that don't change much. These should be automated and predictable.
2. **Financial Goals -** Savings, investments, debt payments—anything that builds long-term financial security. These should also be automated.
3. **Flexible Spending -** Everything else. This is the money left over after financial priorities are handled, and the only rule is **don't spend more than what's available**.

Below is a step-by-step approach to creating a cash-flow-based budgeting system that ensures financial stability while allowing flexibility to spend without guilt.

Step 1 - Determine Monthly Income

The first step in setting up this system is knowing exactly how much money is coming in each month.

For example, take-home pay after taxes might be **$5,000 per month**. This is the starting point of the budget. Always base the budget on after-tax income—what actually lands in the bank account—not the gross salary.

Step 2 - Identify Fixed Costs (50-60% of Income)

Fixed costs include necessary expenses that remain relatively constant each month. These typically include rent or mortgage payments, utilities, insurance, debt payments, and subscriptions.

A typical breakdown might look like this;

- **Rent & Utilities** - $1,800
- **Health & Car Insurance** - $400
- **Student Loan Payment** - $350
- **Phone & Internet** - $120
- **Subscriptions (Netflix, Spotify, etc.)** - $30

Total Fixed Costs - $2,700 (54% of income)

Fixed costs should stay **below 60%** of income to maintain financial flexibility.

Step 3 - Automate Financial Goals (20-30% of Income)

Before spending on anything else, long-term financial goals must be accounted for. This is where many people go wrong—they try to save after spending rather than saving first.

Setting up automatic transfers immediately after payday ensures that financial priorities are met;

- **Group RRSP Contribution (Employer-Sponsored Retirement Plan)** – $500

- **TFSA Contribution (Tax-Free Savings Account)** – $400
- **High-Interest Savings Account (Emergency Fund)** – $300
- **Investments (Index Funds, ETFs, Real Estate)** – $200
- **Extra Student Loan Payments (to pay off debt faster)** – $100

Total Financial Goals - $1,500 (30% of income)

Automate savings **first**, so there's no temptation to spend before saving.

Step 4 - Determine Flexible Spending (Whatever Is Left)

Once fixed costs and savings are taken care of, the remaining balance becomes guilt-free spending money. This is what makes this budget so effective—there's no need to track every purchase. Instead, spending is simply limited to what's available in the checking account.

Using the numbers above, the leftover amount would be -

Income ($5,000) – Fixed Costs ($2,700) – Financial Goals ($1,500) = $800 left for flexible spending

This covers;

- **Groceries**
- **Dining Out & Takeout**
- **Entertainment & Fun**
- **Shopping & Miscellaneous Expenses**

No need for strict spending categories—just ensure that flexible spending stays within the available balance.

Step 5 - Automate the Process

A well-structured budget should run **automatically**, reducing the need for constant tracking. Here's how to make it effortless -

- **Paycheck is deposited into the checking account.**
- Automatic transfers move money to a **Group RRSP, TFSA, and high-interest savings account** before anything else.
- **Fixed costs (rent, insurance, loans) are on autopay.**
- **Whatever remains in the checking account is available for flexible spending.**

Since savings and financial obligations are handled first, there's no need to worry about overspending. The only thing to check is the checking account balance, ensuring it doesn't dip below zero.

This system works because it gives you control without requiring constant oversight. Your financial goals are covered; first, your essentials are paid for, and whatever is left is yours to spend however you want—without guilt, without spreadsheets, without tracking every dollar.

The Final Shift - Making Budgeting Effortless

There's a common misconception about people who are great with money. The world tends to assume they have superhuman discipline—that they resist impulse purchases, track every dollar, and have spreadsheets color-coded down to the cent. But that's not true. The people who win with money don't have more willpower; they simply have better systems.

In psychology, there's a concept called decision fatigue. It explains why judges hand out harsher sentences late in the day, why dieters cave after hours of resisting sweets, and why people make terrible money decisions when they're overwhelmed. The more choices we have to make in a day, the more our cognitive resources drain. By the time we get to the important decisions, we're running on fumes.

Most budgeting methods fail because they require constant vigilance. They ask you to track every meal, every Amazon purchase, every unexpected expense—and by the time you've entered your 200th transaction, exhaustion sets in.

But the people who are financially successful aren't doing that. Instead, they rely on habits and automation. They set up a system where the right financial decisions happen automatically. Their bills are paid without them thinking about it. Their savings grow while they sleep. They don't check their accounts every day because their system ensures that the right things happen by default.

This is the fundamental mindset shift - Budgeting should not be about discipline. It should feel like a tool that runs silently in the background, making sure you build wealth without stress. The best financial plans are not the ones that require constant maintenance but the ones that free you from thinking about money every day.

The truth is financial success isn't about tracking every dollar. It's about setting up a system that takes care of the important things automatically so you can focus on living your life.

A great budget isn't one you constantly have to manage. A great budget is one that manages itself.

IMPORTANCE
OF
EMERGENCY
FUNDS
EMERGENCY
FUNDS

Chapter 4 - Automation, Psychology, and the Lazy Path to Wealth

On March 12, 2020, *The New York Times* published an article that sent a ripple of quiet panic across the country - "*North America's Economy Is About to Shut Down. Will It Ever Reopen the Same?*" At the time, it felt dramatic. The idea that an entire economy—one of the largest, most resilient in the world—could simply grind to a halt overnight seemed impossible. But by the end of that month, restaurants were boarded up, airlines grounded, and millions of Americans were facing a terrifying reality - they were running out of money.

For 38-year-old Rebecca, a hotel manager in Calgary, that reality hit like a train. For over a decade, she had worked her way up in the hospitality industry, going from front desk receptionist to overseeing operations at one of the city's busiest downtown hotels. Her income was steady, her expenses manageable. She had always meant to save more, but there was always something else demanding attention—an extra weekend getaway, a new phone, dinner with friends. Then COVID arrived.

The layoffs came fast. First, the hotel cut housekeeping staff. Then, it shut down banquet halls, cutting event coordinators and catering services. By the time the lockdowns stretched into April, Rebecca's hours were slashed, and within weeks, she was let go entirely. No warning, no severance—just a final paycheck and instructions on how to file for unemployment.

She had $2,200 in her checking account. Rent was $1,500. The math was brutal.

By June, Rebecca was skipping meals to stretch what little she had left. Unemployment payments were slow and unpredictable, and credit card debt began stacking up. She wasn't alone—by July 2020, over 30 million Americans had filed for unemployment benefits. Many, like Rebecca, had assumed they'd be fine without serious savings. After all, the economy had been strong for years, and life seemed stable.

But stability, as millions learned during COVID, is an illusion.

The irony? If Rebecca had just $5,000 in emergency savings, she would have avoided months of financial stress. She wouldn't have been forced into high-interest credit card debt. She wouldn't have had to borrow money from family. She would have had the breathing room to figure out her next steps.

The lesson was clear - Financial disasters aren't about whether you're smart with money. They're about whether you're prepared. And yet, most people aren't.

A 2020 Federal Reserve report found that 39% of Americans wouldn't be able to cover a $400 emergency without borrowing money. It wasn't just a problem for lower-income workers—middle-class households, even those earning six figures, often lived paycheck to paycheck, assuming tomorrow would look like today.

Rebecca's story is not unusual. It is, in fact, the most common financial story in America.

The Myth of Cutting Lattes vs. The Reality of Financial Systems

For years, personal finance experts have told people the key to saving money is cutting small expenses—the infamous "latte factor." The idea is simple - if you spend $5 on coffee every day, that's $150 per month or $1,800 a year. If you just made coffee at home, you could be rich.

It's a tidy theory. The only problem? It doesn't actually work.

Here's why;

1. **It misses the real problem.** Most people don't struggle financially because they buy coffee. They struggle because their fixed expenses—rent, healthcare, debt—eat up most of their income. Cutting out small luxuries barely moves the needle if your rent is consuming half your paycheck.
2. **It assumes willpower works.** Research in behavioral economics consistently shows that people struggle with self-discipline when it comes to money. Relying on yourself to manually "save" every day is like expecting to lose weight by *remembering* to eat less—it rarely works.
3. **It focuses on the wrong scale.** If your goal is to save more money, the real game-changer isn't skipping lattes—it's optimizing the big decisions -
    - **Where you live** (rent or mortgage costs).
    - **How you manage debt** (credit cards, student loans).
    - **What financial systems you automate.**

Consider this - imagine you cut out coffee for a year and saved $1,800. Not bad.

Now, imagine you refinanced a high-interest loan or moved to a slightly cheaper apartment and saved $300 per month. That's $3,600 a year. And you don't have to think about it every day—it just happens.

Big wins beat small cuts every time.

Why This Matters More Than Ever

The pandemic revealed that financial stability isn't about how much you earn but how prepared you are for the unexpected. This brings us to the single most important financial buffer anyone can build - an emergency fund.

For years, the standard advice on emergency savings has been deceptively simple—save three to six months' worth of expenses, keep it in a high-yield savings account, and only use it for emergencies. While this guidance is technically sound, most people struggle to follow it for two main reasons.

- **The target amount feels unreachable.** If someone's monthly expenses are $4,000, they're expected to save between $12,000 and $24,000—an amount that seems overwhelming for those struggling just to cover rent.
- **Even when people do save, the money often doesn't stay put.** A car breaks down, an unexpected bill arrives, or a family member asks for a "temporary" loan, and suddenly, the emergency fund is gone before it ever serves its intended purpose.

As a result, many either never build one at all or use it up before a true crisis strikes.

The most effective solution is not a single emergency fund but a three-tiered approach that acknowledges the reality that financial emergencies come in different sizes. Some problems are small and manageable, some require real financial buffer, and others—like a prolonged job loss or global crisis—necessitate a substantial backup plan.

Tier 1 - The "Oh My Gosh" Fund ($500–$1,000)

This is the first line of defense—small enough to be built quickly but large enough to handle minor emergencies. It covers things like -

- A flat tire or unexpected car repair.
- An urgent medical co-pay.
- A last-minute flight for a family emergency.

Studies show that nearly 40% of Americans wouldn't be able to cover an unexpected $400 expense without borrowing. This fund ensures that a minor inconvenience doesn't spiral into a major financial problem. It should be easily accessible—kept in a basic savings account or even in cash, since emergencies don't wait for a three-day bank transfer.

Tier 2 - The True Emergency Fund (3 Months' Expenses)

This account is designed to sustain someone through bigger financial shocks -

- Job loss.
- Major medical expenses.
- Large home or car repairs.

Ideally, this should be three months' worth of living expenses—typically between $5,000 and $10,000, depending on personal costs. Unlike the first tier, this money should be kept in a high-yield savings account, separate from a daily checking account to prevent accidental spending, but still liquid enough to access in a crisis.

Why three months? Research shows that the average length of unemployment after a layoff is around 20 weeks—but severance pay, unemployment benefits, or a side income can supplement expenses. This fund acts as a firewall between short-term emergencies and long-term financial damage, preventing reliance on high-interest credit cards or payday loans.

Tier 3 - The Long-Term Security Fund (6+ Months' Expenses)

This is the "worst-case scenario" safety net meant for prolonged financial disruption. It should hold six months' worth of expenses or more and be divided between -

- **A high-yield savings account** for immediate access.
- **Conservative investments (bonds, money market funds, or CDs)** to protect against inflation.

This tier ensures that someone isn't just prepared for emergencies but also positioned for long-term financial resilience. By splitting it between savings and low-risk investments, it balances liquidity with growth, preserving purchasing power over time.

How to Build an Emergency Fund (Without Feeling Overwhelmed)

Building an emergency fund can seem daunting, but the key is to start small and automate the process. One of the easiest ways to save is by setting up automatic transfers before the money even reaches a checking account.

- **Start with just 1% of income.** For someone earning $4,000 a month, this would be $40—an amount small enough to go unnoticed.
- **Increase savings by 1% every few months.** This allows savings to build effortlessly.

Over time, this habit shifts the financial baseline, making saving as natural as paying a bill. Another effective strategy is to direct unexpected income—such as tax refunds, work bonuses, or side gig earnings—into savings. Instead of spending every windfall, setting aside at least half ensures that emergency savings grow without requiring additional sacrifices in daily life.

A $1,200 tax refund, for example, could be split into $600 for immediate savings and $600 for discretionary spending, allowing for both financial responsibility and enjoyment.

To prevent unnecessary spending, the placement of savings matters just as much as the habit of saving itself. The most effective strategy is to keep emergency funds slightly inconvenient to access—far enough to avoid impulse withdrawals but not so far that they're inaccessible in a crisis.

- **Use a different bank for savings** than the one used for daily transactions. This extra step discourages casual withdrawals.
- **Rename savings accounts** within online banking apps. Studies show that people save more when accounts are labeled with specific goals, such as -
    - "Emergency Safety Net"
    - "Future Stability Fund"

This simple mental trick makes it harder to justify spending emergency savings on non-urgent expenses.

Financial crises aren't optional—but panic is. The people who survived the COVID-19 economic downturn without financial devastation weren't necessarily those with the highest salaries or the strictest budgets. They were the ones who had built financial systems that protected them from sudden shocks.

The smartest investors don't just build portfolios—they build financial resilience first. A strong emergency fund allows you to invest with confidence, knowing that short-term fluctuations won't derail your long-term wealth-building strategy.

Now that we've covered how to protect your financial future, it's time to explore how to grow it. Let's move into the next step—making your money work for you through smart, strategic investing.

The Secret Weapon of High-Yield Savings Accounts

For decades, traditional banks have marketed savings accounts as a way to keep your money safe and growing. But here's the hard truth - most savings accounts don't actually help your money grow at all. In fact, they do the opposite.

The average interest rate for a traditional savings account sits at around 0.05%—so low that if you had $10,000 parked in one for an entire year, you'd earn a grand total of… $5. Meanwhile, inflation, which hovers around 2-3% annually (and has been much higher recently), means that the real value of that money is actually shrinking. It's like trying to fill a leaky bucket—you're putting money in, but you're still losing it.

The solution? High-yield savings accounts.

In 2021, during the post-pandemic financial recovery, a software engineer named Alex realized his emergency fund—$15,000 sitting in a big-name bank—was doing almost nothing. A quick online search led him to a high-yield savings account offering 2.0% APY at the time. He moved his savings over, and within a year, that same account earned him $300 in interest instead of the measly $7.50 his previous bank would have given him.

Now, some might argue that $300 isn't life-changing, but consider this - over a decade, that's an additional $3,000 in passive earnings for simply moving money from one account to another. No extra work, no additional risk—just a smarter placement of funds.

This is the common mistake many people make - assuming all savings accounts are the same. They're not. A high-yield account can increase savings growth 10 to 20 times faster than a standard one.

How to Pick the Right High-Yield Savings Account

Not all high-yield savings accounts are created equal. While many online banks offer significantly better rates, some still come with fees or inconvenient withdrawal restrictions. Here's what to look for -

- **No fees.** A savings account should never cost you money. If a bank charges maintenance fees or requires a minimum balance, move on.
- **Interest rates at least 10-20x the national average.** The best high-yield accounts should offer 1.5% to 4% APY, depending on economic conditions.
- **Online banks tend to be better.** Because they don't have the overhead costs of physical branches, they pass on the savings to customers with higher interest rates.

The bottom line - a savings account should be a growth vehicle, not a storage locker. If your current bank isn't paying you meaningful interest, it's time to move your money.

The Automation Hack - Why Willpower Is Overrated

Every day, we make hundreds of tiny financial choices - should I buy coffee? Should I eat out for lunch? Should I move money to my savings? By the time we reach the end of the day, our brains are exhausted, and the easiest decision is always to do nothing. The longer we wait, the less likely we are to take action.

Richard Thaler, a Nobel Prize-winning economist, discovered this firsthand. Early in his career, despite his expertise in finance, he struggled to save money. His solution? Automate everything.

He set up a system where -

- A fixed percentage of his paycheck went directly to savings before he even saw it.
- His savings automatically funneled into a retirement account and an investment fund.

- He never had to decide how much to save—his system did it for him.

The result? He saved five times more than when he tried budgeting manually.

This isn't just a one-off success story—it's a proven formula for financial security. The less effort you require to save, the better you will be at saving.

To replicate this approach, set up a system that moves money before you have a chance to spend it.

1. **Set Up Automatic Transfers -**
    - Every payday, have a portion of your income automatically transferred to a high-yield savings account.
    - If you can't start big, begin with just 1% of your income and increase over time.
2. **Use Round-Up Savings Apps -**
    - Apps like Acorns, Qapital, and Chime round up every purchase to the nearest dollar and invest the spare change.
    - If you spend $4.75 on coffee, the extra $0.25 automatically goes into savings. Over time, these micro-savings add up to hundreds or even thousands of dollars.
3. **Automate Retirement Contributions -**
    - If your employer offers a Group RRSP (Registered Retirement Savings Plan) with matching contributions, max it out—it's free money. Just like a 401(k) in the U.S., a Group RRSP allows employees to contribute a portion of their pre-tax salary to a retirement account,

with employers often matching a percentage of those contributions.
    - Even if you're self-employed, set up an RRSP (Registered Retirement Savings Plan) or TFSA (Tax-Free Savings Account) brokerage account with automatic contributions.

The key takeaway? The less you think about saving, the more you'll actually save. Make it automatic, and your wealth builds itself.

The Invisible Threat - Inflation Is Eating Your Savings

Inflation isn't just a history lesson—it's happening right now. In 2022, inflation spiked above 9%, meaning if your money was sitting in a traditional savings account earning 0.05% interest, you were actually losing 8.95% of your money's value every year.

This is the core problem - people assume that "saving" money means protecting money. But in a world where prices rise every year, keeping cash in a low-interest account means you're guaranteed to lose purchasing power over time.

To stay ahead, you need a **tiered financial strategy** -

- **Short-Term Money → High-Yield Savings Account**
    - Emergency funds and short-term savings should be in high-yield accounts to keep up with inflation.
- **Long-Term Money → Stock Market & Investments**
    - If you don't need the money for at least five years, it should be invested in index funds, real estate, or inflation-protected securities.
- **Debt → Strategic Payoff**

- Paying off high-interest debt (credit cards, payday loans) is just as important as saving because it eliminates guaranteed losses from interest payments.

The biggest mistake people make? Hoarding cash instead of putting it to work. Money sitting in a traditional bank account is not growing—it's shrinking.

If you had to remind yourself to brush your teeth every day, you'd probably forget sometimes. But because it's a habit built into your daily routine, you do it automatically. That's exactly how your savings system should work.

A great financial plan isn't one you obsess over—it's one that quietly builds wealth in the background while you live your life.

Pick one automation from this chapter;

- **Set up an automatic transfer to your savings account.**
- **Increase your retirement contributions by 1%.**
- **Open a high-yield savings account and move your emergency fund.**

It doesn't have to be perfect. Just start. Because the sooner you automate your savings, the less effort it will take—and the more wealth you'll quietly build over time.

The people who build wealth aren't constantly thinking about money. They set up systems that work without their input. So, stop relying on willpower. Stop trying to budget harder. And stop believing that saving money requires constant sacrifice.

Instead, set up a financial system that works for you so you can focus on living your life—while your money takes care of itself.

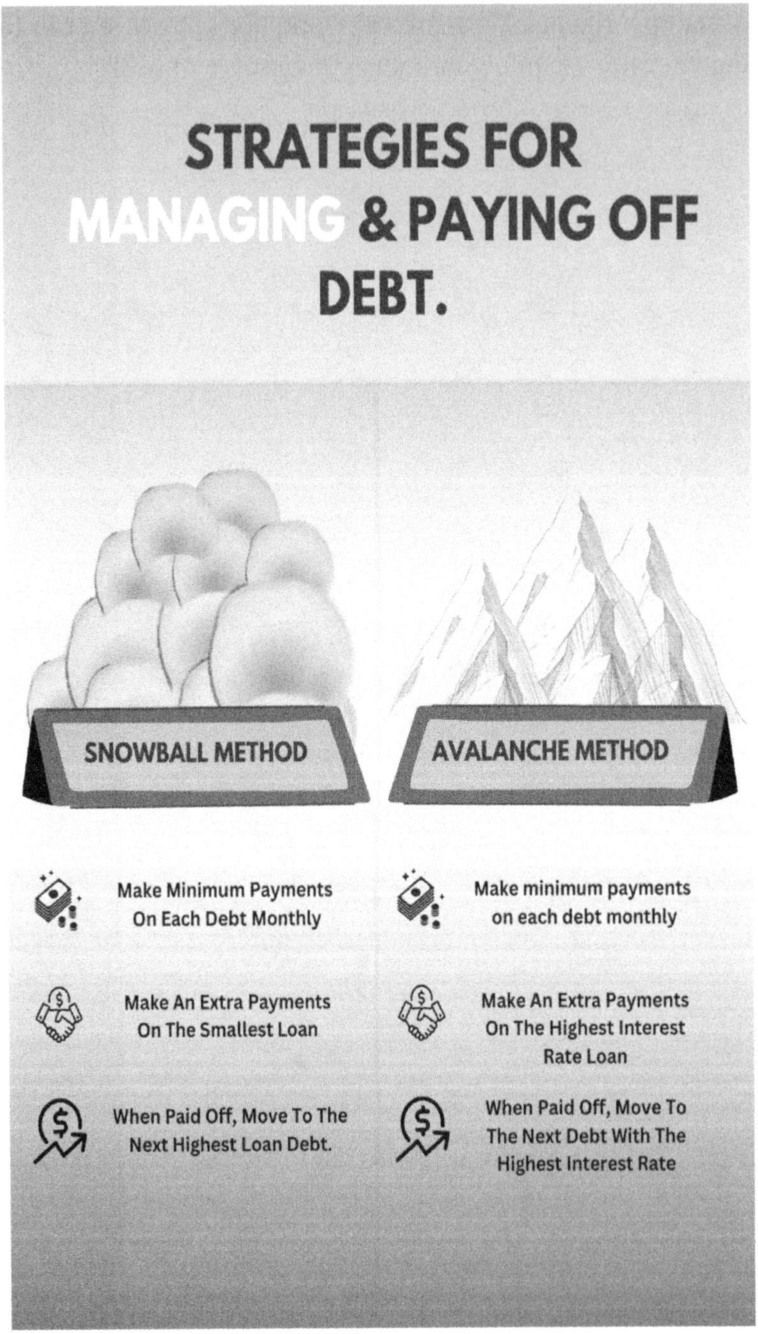
STRATEGIES FOR
MANAGING & PAYING OFF
DEBT.
SNOWBALL METHOD
AVALANCHE METHOD
Make Minimum Payments On Each Debt Monthly
Make minimum payments on each debt monthly
Make An Extra Payments On The Smallest Loan
Make An Extra Payments On The Highest Interest Rate Loan
When Paid Off, Move To The Next Highest Loan Debt.
When Paid Off, Move To The Next Debt With The Highest Interest Rate

Chapter 5 - Breaking Free - The Science of Smart Debt Management

In 1988, a man named Rick Martinez walked into a bank in Toronto with the best credit score of his life. He had just received a promotion, his wife was expecting their first child, and he figured it was time to buy their dream home. The banker smiled, congratulated him, and assured him that he was more than qualified for a mortgage. In fact, the bank pre-approved him for a larger loan than he had ever expected.

At first, Rick hesitated. His budget suggested that a slightly smaller house would be the more responsible choice. But the banker reassured him - *"You have a stable career, you'll be earning more in a few years, and real estate always goes up. You'd be throwing money away by waiting."* That sealed the deal. He signed the paperwork, moved in, and life felt perfect—until it wasn't.

Three years later, Rick's company downsized. He was laid off with little warning, just as the economy was starting to slow down. Suddenly, the mortgage that had once felt like a smart investment became an unbearable weight. With no emergency savings and a second child on the way, Rick did what many in his position do—he turned to credit cards.

At first, it was just to cover groceries and utilities until he could find another job. Then, as months passed, the balances grew. Interest piled up. His new job paid less than his last, and soon, the minimum payments alone were draining his paycheck.

Rick's story isn't unique. The details change, but the pattern repeats itself across generations. A person who seems financially stable today can find themselves drowning in debt within a few short years. Not because they were reckless but because they made one seemingly logical decision at the wrong time. We like to believe that debt only happens to people who are irresponsible with money. In reality, the financial system is designed to encourage borrowing. Banks profit when you take on debt, so they create incentives—bigger credit limits, low introductory interest rates, deferred payments—to make borrowing feel like a natural part of life. And when people do run into trouble? The solution they're offered is often… *more debt.*

That's why debt isn't just a numbers game—it's a psychological trap. And getting out of it has less to do with budgeting harder and more to do with understanding why we borrow in the first place.

The Psychology of Debt - Why We Borrow Even When We Shouldn't

In 1957, economist Milton Friedman introduced the **"permanent income hypothesis."** His idea was simple - people don't just spend based on what they earn today—they spend based on what they *expect* to earn in the future.

This explains why people feel comfortable taking on debt even when they don't have the money to repay it today. They assume that *future them*—who will have a better job, higher income, and more stability—will handle it easily. It's an optimistic way to look at money. And in some cases, it's true. Many people do see their incomes rise over time. But for those who don't? Debt becomes a permanent fixture of their financial lives.

Psychologists have a name for this mistake - optimism bias. It's the reason why we assume we'll be better off in the future, even when there's no concrete evidence to support it. This bias doesn't just affect individuals. It affects entire economies.

Take the housing crash of 2008. Millions of people took on massive mortgages because they believed home prices would always go up. When the bubble burst, families who had once been "smart investors" found themselves buried in debt they could never repay.

The same thing happens at the individual level every day. People swipe credit cards because they assume they'll be able to pay them off next month. They finance cars under the belief that they'll get a raise soon. They take out student loans, believing that all degrees lead to higher salaries.

But what if those assumptions are wrong?

That's why escaping debt isn't just about cutting expenses or making a budget. Those things matter, but they don't fix the underlying issue - people don't get into debt because they can't do math. They get into debt because of how they think.

Three Psychological Traps That Keep People in Debt

1. **Loss Aversion** – Studies show that people fear losing something more than they value gaining something of equal value. This explains why so many people go into debt to maintain a lifestyle they can't afford. The thought of downsizing their home, driving an older car, or cutting back on luxuries feels like a *loss*—so they choose debt instead.

2. **The Illusion of Minimum Payments** – Credit card companies make debt look manageable by offering low minimum payments. What they don't advertise is that making only the minimum payment on a $5,000 credit card balance at 20% interest will take over 30 years to pay off. People assume they're staying on top of their finances when, in reality, they're trapped in a cycle designed to extract as much money as possible from them.

3. **Decision Fatigue** – The more financial choices we have to make, the worse we get at making them. Research has shown that when people are constantly bombarded with financial decisions, they default to the easiest option—which, for most, is doing nothing and continuing to make the minimum payments. This is why people stay in debt far longer than they should.

The key to breaking free from debt isn't just knowing that these psychological traps exist—it's building a system that bypasses them entirely.

That's where understanding different types of debt comes in. Because not all debt is created equal. Some types are meant to be paid off quickly. Others can be leveraged to your advantage. Knowing the difference is what separates those who stay trapped in debt from those who use it as a tool for financial growth.

The Hidden Trap of Debt - Not All Loans Are the Same

Not all debt is created equal. Some types of loans help build wealth, while others act like financial quicksand. The key to managing debt isn't just about paying it off—it's about knowing which debts are worth keeping and which need to be eliminated immediately. The biggest mistake people make is treating all loans the same, failing to recognize that some work against them far more aggressively than others.

Credit card debt is one of the worst kinds of debt to carry because of its high interest rates and compounding structure. Unlike a mortgage or student loan, which comes with fixed monthly payments and lower interest rates, credit cards are designed to make you pay as long as possible. If you carry a $5,000 balance on a credit card with a 20% interest rate and only make the minimum payments, it could take over 30 years to pay off. That's longer than most home mortgages. Interest compounds daily, meaning every day, your balance grows larger. And because many people only pay the minimum amount due, the debt doesn't just linger—it multiplies.

Student loans operate differently, though they can still become overwhelming if not managed properly. Federal student loans offer fixed interest rates and more flexible repayment options, including income-driven repayment plans that adjust based on your salary. Some even come with loan forgiveness programs if you work in certain public service roles. Private student loans, however, often lack these protections, carrying variable interest rates that can rise over time. While student loans can be an investment in the future, they require careful planning. Borrowing more than necessary or neglecting to research repayment options can lead to years of financial strain.

Mortgages and auto loans fall into a separate category because they are secured debt, meaning they are backed by collateral. If you default on your mortgage, the bank can take your house. If you stop making car payments, your vehicle can be repossessed. The good news is that because these loans are secured, they usually come with much lower interest rates than credit cards or personal loans. A mortgage with a 3% or 5% interest rate is significantly different from a credit card charging

20% or more. That's why mortgage debt—when managed properly—is often considered "good debt." You're building equity in a home, an asset that can appreciate over time. Auto loans, on the other hand, are trickier. Cars depreciate the moment they're driven off the lot, meaning the debt you owe on a car often exceeds its value within just a few years.

Then there's personal loans, which are often used for debt consolidation, medical bills, or large purchases. These loans are unsecured, meaning there's no collateral backing them up. Because of that, lenders charge higher interest rates, though still lower than what most credit cards demand. Used wisely, personal loans can be a tool to consolidate higher-interest debt, lowering overall monthly payments. But used recklessly, they can add to financial burdens, particularly if they're taken out without a clear repayment plan.

The bottom line - not all debt is equal, and understanding the differences between them is key. Credit card debt should be eliminated as quickly as possible, student loans need strategic repayment planning, mortgages can be leveraged for long-term wealth, and auto loans should be approached with caution. Most financial stress doesn't come from having debt—it comes from having the wrong kind of debt at the wrong time.

How to Escape Debt - The Two Winning Strategies (With Real Examples)

Once you've identified which debts are hurting you the most, the next step is to pay them off strategically. The two most effective methods—the Snowball Method and the Avalanche Method—both work, but in very different ways.

The Snowball Method focuses on paying off your smallest debts first, regardless of their interest rates. The logic behind this approach is simple - small wins keep you motivated. When people see one balance disappear, they feel a sense of progress, making it easier to stay disciplined. This method works well for those who need psychological momentum. It's the financial equivalent of decluttering a messy house—tackling the smallest pile first makes the overall task feel more manageable.

Imagine Sarah has the following debts -

- **$600** on a store credit card (**24% interest rate**)
- **$2,500** on a personal loan (**10% interest rate**)
- **$7,000** in student loans (**5% interest rate**)

Using the Snowball Method, Sarah would ignore the interest rates and focus on the smallest balance first. She puts as much extra money as possible toward the $600 store credit card while making minimum payments on the other debts. In just a few months, that card is paid off.

Now, Sarah takes the money she was paying toward the store card and applies it to the $2,500 personal loan, accelerating her payments. Once that's cleared, she finally attacks the $7,000 student loan. Even though she might have paid a little more in interest by ignoring the highest rates, the psychological wins kept her engaged and helped her eliminate debt much faster than if she had lost motivation along the way.

On the other hand, the Avalanche Method prioritizes paying off the debts with the highest interest rates first. This method is mathematically superior because it minimizes the total interest paid over time. If you have a credit card with a 22% interest rate and a student loan with a 6% interest rate, the Avalanche Method directs all extra payments to the credit card first since that's where interest accumulates the fastest. The downside? It can take longer to see significant results, which may make it harder to stay motivated.

Now let's look at Mark's situation -

- **$4,000** in credit card debt (**22% interest rate**)
- **$10,000** in auto loan debt (**8% interest rate**)
- **$20,000** in student loans (**5% interest rate**)

Using the Avalanche Method, Jason focuses on the $4,000 credit card debt first since it has the highest interest rate. Even though his auto loan balance is smaller, its lower interest rate means it's costing him less over time. By eliminating his high-interest credit card first, Jason saves hundreds or even thousands in extra interest payments.

Once the credit card is cleared, he applies all extra funds toward the $10,000 auto loan. With that out of the way, he finally tackles his $20,000 student loan, the lowest-interest debt in his lineup. While it might take longer for him to see a zero balance on his first debt, he pays far less in interest than if he had tackled the debts smallest-to-largest.

Both strategies have merit, and choosing the right one depends on personality and financial discipline.

- If staying motivated is the biggest challenge, the Snowball Method is effective.
- If saving the most money over time is the priority, the Avalanche Method is better.

- Some people even use a hybrid approach—starting with the Snowball Method to build momentum and switching to the Avalanche Method once they feel more confident.

Regardless of the approach, consistency is key. Missing payments or making only minimum payments will keep you stuck in debt indefinitely. The most effective strategy is the one that keeps you engaged long enough to reach the finish line.

The Truth About Debt Consolidation & Refinancing

Debt consolidation sounds like a financial cure-all. You take all your existing loans—credit card balances, personal loans, student loans—and roll them into one easy payment with a lower interest rate. On paper, it looks like a dream. But is it actually the smart move?

The reality is, debt consolidation can either be a lifeline or a trap, depending on how and when you do it. Too often, people use consolidation to mask financial problems rather than solve them. If you're drowning in debt because of overspending, rolling everything into one neat package won't fix the root issue. It's like rearranging the deck chairs on the Titanic—it looks better, but you're still sinking.

So when does consolidation actually make sense? When it truly lowers your interest rate and helps you pay off debt faster. If you have multiple high-interest debts (say, credit cards with rates of 20% or higher), consolidating into a lower-interest personal loan or balance transfer card can save you thousands. But this only works if you avoid accumulating more debt while paying off the consolidated loan. Otherwise, you'll end up right back where you started—only now with even more debt.

Refinancing, on the other hand, is a more targeted approach—you're not rolling all your debts into one; you're replacing a high-interest loan with a lower-interest one. This is especially useful for -

- **Mortgages** (getting a lower rate can save you tens of thousands over the life of the loan).
- **Student loans** (federal loans have better protections, but private loans can often be refinanced at better rates).
- **Auto loans** (if you got a bad deal when you bought the car, refinancing can save you big).
- **Personal loans** (if your credit score has improved, refinancing can lower your payments).

The Hidden Traps of Debt Consolidation

Most people don't realize that debt consolidation companies make money off fees, and not all consolidation loans actually save you money. Here are the biggest pitfalls to watch for -

- **Origination Fees** – Some lenders charge 3-5% just to process your new consolidated loan. That means if you're rolling $20,000 into a loan, you could lose $600-$1,000 before you even make a payment.
- **Longer Terms = More Interest** – A lower monthly payment feels great—until you realize you're now paying for 10 years instead of 5. Even with a lower interest rate, stretching out the loan means paying more overall.
- **Teaser Rates That Disappear** – Some balance transfer credit cards offer 0% APR for 12-18 months, which sounds amazing—until you miss a payment and suddenly get hit with a 25% penalty rate.

Let's look at two people who approached refinancing in very different ways.

Tom made a classic mistake. He had $15,000 in credit card debt spread across three cards, all with interest rates around 21%. He decided to consolidate into a single personal loan at 12% interest, thinking he'd solved his problem. But once his credit card balances were wiped clean, he went right back to using them—and within a year, he had racked up another $10,000 in new debt. Now, he was making payments on both the consolidation loan and new credit card balances—doubling his financial burden.

Samantha played it differently. She also had $15,000 in credit card debt, but instead of taking out a personal loan, she transferred her balance to a 0% APR credit card. She aggressively paid off $3,000 per month and cleared the full balance before the promo rate expired. By taking advantage of a strategic refinancing move, she eliminated her debt without paying a dime in interest.

The difference? Samantha had a plan. Tom just moved money around without changing his behavior.

So before jumping into consolidation or refinancing, ask yourself -

1. **Am I solving the problem or just moving debt around?**
2. **Do I have a plan to pay off the loan before I take on new debt?**
3. **Am I watching out for hidden fees or risky terms?**

If you don't have a plan, consolidation won't save you—it will just **prolong your debt sentence.**

The Negotiation Hack - How to Reduce Interest Rates Without Refinancing

Most people assume that interest rates are set in stone. If your credit card charges 20% APR, that's just the cost of borrowing, right?

Wrong.

Banks rely on the fact that most people never even try to negotiate their rates. They assume borrowers will accept whatever they're given. But here's the truth - your interest rate is negotiable, and a five-minute phone call could save you hundreds or even thousands of dollars.

David had been carrying a $8,000 balance on his credit card, paying 19% interest. One day, he read that banks are more likely to lower rates for customers who simply ask.

So he picked up the phone and said -

> *"Hi, I've been a loyal customer for five years, and I'd like to request a lower interest rate. I've received offers from other banks with better rates, but I'd prefer to stay with you. Can you match their offer?"*

At first, the representative hesitated, but when David mentioned other offers, they immediately dropped his rate from 19% to 12%. That simple negotiation saved him over $500 in interest that year alone.

Step-By-Step Script to Negotiate a Lower Rate

If you have a credit card balance, try this;

1. **Call customer service.** (Choose "speak to a representative" instead of automated options).
2. **Be polite, but firm.** Say -
    - *"I've been a customer for [X] years, and I'd like to lower my interest rate."*
    - *"I've received competing offers with lower rates. Can you match or beat them?"*
3. **If they say no, ask for a supervisor.** Customer reps have limited authority—managers can often approve better deals.
4. **If they still say no, ask - "What would I need to do to qualify?"** Sometimes, just improving your payment history for a few months can get you a better rate.

Why Don't More People Try This?

- **Fear of rejection** – People assume they'll get a flat "no," so they never ask.
- **They don't know it's possible** – Credit card companies won't advertise this option, because they profit from higher rates.
- **They don't think it matters** – But even a **2-5% reduction** in your APR can save **hundreds of dollars per year.**

If one company won't budge, shop around. Many banks offer promotional balance transfers with 0% interest for 12-18 months. Transferring your balance to a lower-rate card is another way to cut your interest costs overnight.

The Final Shift - Automating Debt Freedom

This is the real secret behind debt freedom - it's not about self-control—it's about systems. If you have to remind yourself to make an extra payment every month, or if you're constantly deciding between spending and paying off debt, you're setting yourself up for failure. Your brain is wired to avoid discomfort, and every manual debt payment is a reminder of financial stress. That's why most people fail—they exhaust their willpower before they see results.

Instead, the solution is simple - set up an automatic system that eliminates debt in the background without you thinking about it.

1. **Auto-pay the minimums** on all debts to avoid late fees and penalties. Never let a missed payment damage your credit score.
2. **Auto-transfer extra payments** toward your highest-priority debt. Whether you're using the Snowball Method (smallest to largest debts) or Avalanche Method (highest interest first), set up automatic transfers so the extra payments happen before you can spend the money elsewhere.
3. **Redirect money from paid-off debts into savings or investments.** This is how you prevent "lifestyle inflation"—the trap where people free up money by paying off debt but then immediately spend it on something else. Instead, take the same payment amount and redirect it into savings or investing.

Here's the final, counterintuitive truth - debt isn't the enemy. It's just a tool. Used recklessly, it can burn you—like fire. Used wisely, it can build wealth, open doors, and create opportunities.

The real goal isn't just to get out of debt—it's to take control of it. Most people think of debt as something to escape from, but financially successful people see it as something to manage, leverage, and master. A mortgage can build wealth. A business loan can create opportunities. A strategic credit move can save thousands. The key is understanding the difference between good debt and bad debt—and making debt work for you, not against you.

So here's your challenge -

- Don't just eliminate debt. Eliminate financial stress.
- Don't just avoid borrowing. Learn how to borrow wisely.
- Don't just focus on paying off loans. Focus on building wealth.

In the next chapter, we'll take the next step - now that debt isn't a burden, how do you turn your money into real, lasting wealth?

UNDERSTANDING CREDIT SCORES AND THEIR COMPONENTS
HIGH CREDIT SCORE

Chapter 6 – The Credit Code - Unlocking Your Financial Reputation

In 2019, two men applied for mortgages. Both had stable jobs, similar incomes, and were looking at homes in the same price range. The only difference? Their credit scores.

Jake, with a credit score of 790, secured a 30-year fixed mortgage at 2.8% interest. His monthly payment was $1,650. Carlos, with a credit score of 610, was approved—but at 6.5% interest. His monthly payment for the same house? $2,150—$500 more per month, or an extra $180,000 over the life of the loan.

Carlos didn't think much about his credit score. He assumed it was just a number that determined whether he could borrow money. What he didn't realize was that his credit score was dictating the cost of his financial life. He wasn't just paying more for his mortgage—he was also paying higher interest on his car loan, getting denied for the best credit cards, and even facing higher insurance premiums.

Most people assume credit scores only matter when they need to borrow money. But that's a mistake. Landlords use them to decide who gets approved for apartments. Employers in certain industries check them before making a job offer. Insurance companies factor them into their pricing models, which means that even something as simple as car insurance can be more expensive if your credit score isn't where it should be.

Here's the counterintuitive truth - A credit score isn't about whether you can borrow money—it's about how much life will cost you. If you don't take control of it, you'll quietly bleed thousands of dollars over the years, often without realizing it. But once you understand how it works, you can turn it into a tool that saves you money instead of draining your wallet.

Understanding the Credit Score Formula

If your financial life were a video game, your credit score would be your reputation meter. And just like in any game, every action you take—every bill you pay, every loan you apply for—either strengthens or weakens your standing. The system may seem mysterious, but in reality, it follows a strict formula.

Your credit score is built on five key factors, each weighted differently -

1. Payment History (35%) – The Make-or-Break Factor

The biggest chunk of your credit score comes down to one simple question - Do you pay your bills on time? This is the first thing lenders check, and even a single missed payment can have long-term consequences.

A late payment stays on your credit report for seven years. Even if you catch up a few days later, the damage is done. The more recent the late payment, the worse the impact—miss a payment this month, and your score could drop 50 to 100 points overnight.

But here's the catch - The system rewards consistency more than perfection. If you've missed a payment in the past but build a long streak of on-time payments, your score will start climbing again.

2. Credit Utilization (30%) – The Balancing Act

Imagine you have a $10,000 credit limit spread across multiple cards. If you're carrying a balance of $7,500, that means you're using 75% of your available credit. In the eyes of credit bureaus, that's a red flag. It signals that you might be relying too much on borrowed money.

The ideal utilization rate? Below 30%. If you can keep it under 10%, even better.

Most people assume that paying off their credit cards in full every month is all that matters. But utilization is calculated based on your statement balance, not just your payments. That means if your balance is high when the credit card company reports it to the bureaus—even if you pay it off right after—you'll still look like you're overextended.

3. Length of Credit History (15%) – The Slow Burn

Lenders like to see a long, stable track record. The longer you've had credit, the better your score. This is why closing old credit cards can actually hurt you. When you shut down a card you've had for 10 years, you shorten your average account age—potentially lowering your score in the process.

This is where a lot of well-intentioned financial advice goes wrong. People are told to close unused credit cards to "clean up" their finances. But unless the card has a hefty annual fee, leave it open—even if you don't use it often. The length of your credit history isn't something you can fix overnight, but it's one of the simplest ways to keep your score strong over time.

4. Credit Mix (10%) – The Diversity Factor

If you only have credit cards, your score might be lower than someone with a mix of different credit types—like a mortgage, a student loan, and a car loan. Lenders like to see that you can handle different types of debt responsibly.

That doesn't mean you should go out and take on debt just to improve your score. But if you're thinking about taking out an installment loan—like a car loan or a small personal loan—it could actually help your credit in the long run by adding diversity to your credit profile.

5. New Credit Inquiries (10%) – The Red Flag

Every time you apply for a new loan or credit card, the lender performs a hard inquiry on your credit report. One or two inquiries won't hurt much, but applying for multiple credit cards at once can lower your score.

Think of it from a lender's perspective - If someone suddenly applies for five new credit cards in a month, it looks like they might be in financial trouble. This is why spacing out credit applications is important.

The exception? If you're shopping around for a mortgage or an auto loan, credit bureaus recognize that you're rate shopping, so multiple inquiries within a short window (typically 14–45 days) count as one inquiry instead of several.

What Lenders See (and What You Should Check)

For most people, a credit report is just another bureaucratic document—until they need a loan. Suddenly, this obscure record determines whether they can buy a home, get a car, or even secure a job in certain industries. But what most people don't realize is that one in five credit reports contains an error, and those errors can cost you thousands of dollars in higher interest rates or outright rejections from lenders.

Imagine applying for a mortgage after years of careful financial planning. Your income is stable, you've saved a decent down payment, and your credit score seems fine. Then, the bank denies your application. Why? Because of a collections account you didn't even know existed. Maybe it was an old medical bill that got lost in the shuffle, or worse, a fraudulent account opened in your name. You never saw it coming, but the lender did—and to them, it's a red flag.

This happens all the time, yet most people only check their credit reports after a problem arises. But by then, fixing errors takes time—time you may not have when you're trying to secure a loan. The reality is, you need to review your credit report regularly, not just when you're about to make a big financial move.

Every credit report is maintained by three major bureaus - Experian, Equifax, and TransUnion. These companies collect data from lenders, compiling a record of how you manage debt. When you apply for a loan or a credit card, banks pull this report to determine your risk level.

By law, you're entitled to one free credit report per year from each bureau, which you can access at AnnualCreditReport.com. That means you can check one every four months—Experian in January,

TransUnion in May, Equifax in September—to keep tabs on your credit throughout the year. This staggered approach ensures you don't go too long without checking.

Some companies try to charge for credit reports, bundling them with "monitoring services" or "identity theft protection." These services aren't always scams, but you don't need to pay for your basic credit report. Many banks and credit card issuers now offer free credit monitoring as part of their services, so check if yours does before signing up for anything.

How to Read Your Credit Report Like a Lender

Getting your credit report is one thing—understanding it is another. Lenders don't just glance at your score; they analyze specific sections to assess how reliable you are. When you review your report, think like a lender and focus on these key areas.

First, check your personal information. This includes your name, address, Social Security number, and employment history. Even minor errors, like an address you never lived at, can indicate potential identity theft. If you see information that doesn't belong to you, flag it immediately.

Next, review your credit accounts—both open and closed. This section details every line of credit in your name, from credit cards to auto loans. Ensure that balances are accurate and that old accounts are marked as closed if they should be. If a creditor is reporting the wrong balance, it could be dragging down your score. Your payment history is the most important part of your report. Late payments, missed payments, and accounts sent to collections stay on your record for years. If you see a late payment that you know was made on time, dispute it immediately—even a single mistake could be costing you points.

Another section to watch is credit inquiries. When you apply for new credit, lenders perform a hard inquiry, which can temporarily lower your score. If you see inquiries you don't recognize, it could mean someone is applying for credit in your name. Soft inquiries—when you check your own credit or get pre-approved for offers—don't affect your score, but they should still be accurate.

Check public records, which include bankruptcies, foreclosures, and tax liens. These have a serious impact on your credit score and remain on your report for years. If any of these records appear incorrectly, they must be addressed immediately.

How to Fix Errors (Before They Cost You Thousands)

Errors on your credit report won't fix themselves, and lenders won't take your word for it if you claim a mistake has been made. You have to be proactive.

First, gather evidence—bank statements, payment confirmations, or any documents that prove the error. Then, file a dispute with the credit bureau that's reporting the incorrect information. This can be done online, by phone, or through the mail, but online disputes are generally the fastest.

The credit bureau has 30 days to investigate. If they find an error, they'll correct it and send you an updated report. But don't assume the issue is resolved—follow up to ensure the mistake is removed from all three credit bureaus.

Once your report is accurate, set up a habit of checking it regularly. Fixing a mistake now can mean a higher credit score, lower interest rates, and better financial opportunities down the line.

How to Boost Your Credit Score Quickly

Building good credit is a long-term game, but if you need a boost fast—say, to qualify for a mortgage or auto loan—there are proven strategies to raise your score in weeks, not years.

One trick is paying your credit card bill twice a month instead of once. Credit scores are heavily influenced by your credit utilization ratio, which measures how much of your available credit you're using. Paying down your balance before your statement closes lowers your reported utilization, improving your score almost instantly.

Another method is the "15% Rule" for credit utilization. Ideally, you should never use more than 30% of your available credit, but the best scores come from those who keep balances under 15%. If your limit is $10,000, that means staying under $1,500 in usage at all times. If your balance is already high, paying down some of it before your statement closes can help.

A lesser-known strategy is becoming an authorized user on someone else's credit card. If a family member with excellent credit adds you to their account, their credit history gets added to yours—potentially boosting your score overnight. The key is making sure the account has a long, clean history.

Many people hurt their credit by closing old accounts, thinking it's the responsible thing to do. But this actually shortens your credit history and increases your utilization ratio, both of which can lower your score.

Unless an old account has high fees, keep it open—even if you don't use it.

The biggest credit mistakes usually happen because people don't understand how scoring works. One common trap is opening store credit cards just for discounts. That 10% off might not be worth the hard inquiry and lower average account age that come with opening a new card. Another mistake is ignoring errors on your credit report for too long. Disputing errors takes time, and waiting until you need a loan to fix them is risky. Even if you don't plan on applying for credit soon, keeping your report accurate ensures you're always prepared.

Avoid applying for multiple new credit cards at once. Each application creates a hard inquiry, and too many in a short period can make you look desperate for credit—a red flag for lenders.

Credit Myths That Cost People Thousands

One of the biggest obstacles to good credit isn't a lack of knowledge—it's misinformation. Credit myths circulate like urban legends, passed down by well-meaning parents, outdated financial advisors, and even banks that profit from keeping consumers confused. These myths don't just create bad habits; they cost people thousands in unnecessary interest payments, fees, and lost opportunities. Let's debunk some of the most damaging ones.

Myth #1 - Carrying a Small Balance Improves Your Score

This is one of the most expensive myths out there, and credit card companies love it. The idea is that keeping a small balance on your card (instead of paying it off in full) somehow signals to lenders that you're a "responsible borrower," boosting your score.

Reality check - This is completely false. Your credit score is calculated based on your credit utilization—the percentage of your available credit that you're using. If you carry a balance, you're increasing your utilization ratio, which can lower your score, not improve it.

Even worse, carrying a balance means you're paying interest unnecessarily. Credit card companies make billions off people who believe this myth, trapping them in an endless cycle of interest payments that could have been avoided by simply paying off the balance in full every month.

What to do instead - Always pay your credit card in full before the statement due date. This shows lenders you can manage credit responsibly without racking up unnecessary debt.

Myth #2 - Closing a Credit Card Erases Your History

Many people believe that if they close an old credit card account, it will remove that card's history from their report—especially if they made some mistakes on it in the past. But that's not how credit reports work.

Your credit history isn't erased when you close an account. Instead, closing an old account can actually lower your credit score in two ways -

1. **It shortens your credit history** – Credit scores reward long, stable credit relationships. When you close an old account, your average account age decreases, which can hurt your score.
2. **It increases your credit utilization ratio** – Let's say you have three credit cards with a total credit limit of $20,000. If you close one with a $5,000 limit, your total available credit drops

to $15,000, increasing your credit utilization ratio and potentially lowering your score.

What to do instead - Keep old credit cards open unless they have high annual fees. If you don't use them, consider putting a small, recurring charge on the card (like a streaming subscription) and setting up automatic payments to keep it active.

Myth #3 - A High Income Equals a High Credit Score

People assume that if they make six figures, they'll automatically have an excellent credit score. After all, banks love high earners, right?

Not exactly. Your income isn't even a factor in your credit score. A person making $40,000 a year who pays their bills on time and keeps their credit utilization low will have a better credit score than someone making $200,000 who maxes out their cards and misses payments.

Lenders don't judge your creditworthiness by how much you earn—they judge it by how well you manage the credit you have. Someone with a modest salary but a strong repayment history will always have better borrowing power than a high-income earner with poor credit habits.

What to do instead - Focus on payment history and debt management, not income. If you get a raise, use it to pay down existing debt or boost savings instead of increasing spending.

Myth #4 - You Only Have One Credit Score

Most people think their credit score is a single, fixed number, like a grade on a test. But in reality, you have multiple credit scores, and the number you see may not be the one a lender sees.

There are different scoring models, the most common being FICO and VantageScore. Within FICO alone, there are different versions used for mortgages, auto loans, and credit cards. So, while you might check your score through a free service and see a 750, a mortgage lender might pull a different version of your FICO score and see a 720.

What to do instead - Don't fixate on a single number. Instead, focus on good credit habits—paying bills on time, keeping utilization low, and avoiding unnecessary hard inquiries. If you maintain strong financial behavior, all versions of your score will remain in good standing.

Why a Good Credit Score Isn't Enough (And What Comes Next)

Think of a credit score like a passport. A passport doesn't guarantee you a great vacation—it just gives you access to more destinations. Similarly, a high credit score doesn't automatically make you financially successful, but it opens doors - lower interest rates, better loan terms, and even business opportunities. The real question is, what do you do with that access?

Most financial advice treats credit like a danger zone—something to be avoided, managed, or escaped from. But the most successful people don't just avoid bad credit—they leverage good credit to create wealth.

Instead of thinking of credit as a personal trap, think of it as a financial tool. Used wisely, it can -

- **Help you buy appreciating assets** – A mortgage with a low interest rate lets you buy real estate, which can grow in value over time.

- **Fund a business or investment** – Entrepreneurs use business lines of credit to scale operations without using their own cash.
- **Provide financial flexibility** – Good credit means lower borrowing costs when opportunities arise, like investing in property or funding education.

But here's the key - Credit only works in your favor if it's used strategically. Taking on debt for lifestyle inflation—bigger houses, fancier cars, or luxury vacations—won't build wealth. But, leveraging debt for assets that grow in value can change your financial future.

So, you've mastered your credit score. You know how it's calculated, how to check your report, and how to avoid the myths that trip people up. Now comes the real question - How do you move beyond a good credit score to financial independence?

That's what the next chapter is about. Because credit alone doesn't make you rich—it's how you use it that determines your financial future.

SIMPLIFYING INVESTMENT

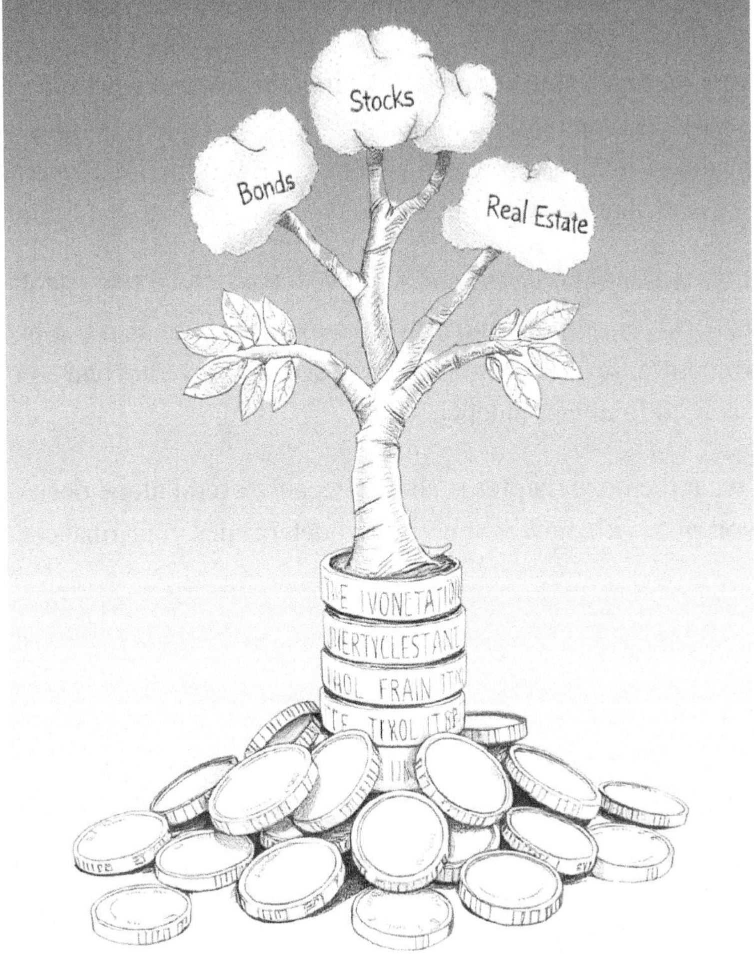

CONCEPTS FOR BEGINNERS

Chapter 7 - Investing for Beginners—How to Make Your Money Work for You

In 1972, a gas station attendant named Ronald Read made a decision that would change his life. It wasn't dramatic. He didn't start a business, land a six-figure salary, or inherit a fortune. Instead, he did something so unremarkable that most people wouldn't even notice - he started investing a small portion of his paycheck every month.

Ronald Read never made more than a modest salary. He pumped gas, swept floors, and lived frugally. He wore old flannel shirts, drove an aging car, and was the kind of man who fixed his own plumbing to save a few dollars. When he died in 2014 at the age of 92, his friends and neighbors were stunned to learn that the quiet janitor had accumulated over $8 million in investments.

Meanwhile, at the other end of the wealth spectrum, celebrities, athletes, and even financial professionals with six-figure salaries were going bankrupt.

How?

Because investing isn't about how much you earn—it's about what you do with what you earn. For decades, people have been told that investing is complicated, that it's for the rich, that it requires market timing or advanced financial knowledge. But Ronald Read's story proves that none of that is true. The real key to wealth isn't earning more—it's making your money work for you. And to do that, you only need to understand three types of investments.

The Three Investments You Need to Understand

Most people believe investing is complex, filled with confusing jargon and high-risk bets. The truth is, investing is actually much simpler than most financial advisors want you to believe. At its core, there are only three main investments that matter - stocks, bonds, and funds. If you understand how these three work, you'll be ahead of 90% of investors.

Stocks - Owning a Piece of a Business

Imagine you walk into your favorite coffee shop one day, and the owner tells you he's looking for investors. He offers you a deal - if you give him $1,000, he'll give you a small share of the business. If the coffee shop does well, your share grows in value. If it struggles, your investment shrinks.

That's exactly how stocks work.

When you buy a stock, you're buying a small ownership stake in a company. If the company grows, your investment grows. If it declines, so does your money. Some companies even pay you a portion of their profits in the form of dividends—essentially rewarding you just for being an investor.

Stocks offer the highest long-term returns of any investment. Historically, the stock market has returned about 7–10% annually over long periods. That means if you invest $10,000 today, it could grow to over $70,000 in 25 years without you lifting a finger. Stocks are risky. The value of your shares can rise and fall dramatically. Some companies go bankrupt. That's why smart investors don't put all their money in one stock—they spread it across multiple companies.

Bonds - Lending Money and Earning Interest

If stocks are about owning a business, bonds are about lending money—but on your terms. Think about it like this - imagine a friend needs $5,000 to start a bakery, but he doesn't want to give up ownership. Instead, he asks to borrow the money and promises to pay you back with interest.

That's exactly what bonds are. You're lending money to a company or government, and in return, they pay you interest. Bonds are safer than stocks because they guarantee a fixed return. Even if a company struggles, they are legally required to pay their bondholders before they pay their stockholders. This makes bonds an excellent choice for stability and consistent income.

But there's a trade-off - bonds grow wealth more slowly. While stocks can return 7–10% a year, bonds typically return 3–5%. That's why most investors use them as a balance—to reduce risk while still earning steady returns.

Mutual Funds & ETFs - The Lazy Investor's Dream

Let's say you want to invest in stocks but don't want to spend hours researching individual companies. Enter mutual funds and ETFs—the easiest way to invest without becoming an expert. Think of a mutual fund like a personal shopper for investments. Instead of picking stocks yourself, you hire a professional to manage your money and choose stocks for you. Your money gets pooled with other investors, and the fund manager invests in a wide range of companies.

An ETF (Exchange-Traded Fund) is even simpler. Imagine walking into a grocery store and grabbing a pre-made basket labeled "Tech Stocks" or "Healthcare Companies." Instead of buying individual stocks, you buy a bundle of them all at once. The beauty of mutual funds and ETFs? They let you invest in hundreds of companies at once—giving you instant diversification with zero effort.

The best investors use funds strategically to spread their risk and save time. Instead of obsessing over stock picks, they simply invest in a broad, low-cost index fund that follows the entire market. Historically, index funds have beaten most professional stock pickers over the long run.

Ronald Read didn't get rich picking stocks. He didn't have an MBA. He wasn't following daily market news.

Instead, he followed **three simple rules** -

1. **He invested consistently.** No matter how small the amount, he put money into the market every month.
2. **He diversified.** Instead of betting everything on one company, he owned a wide range of stocks and bonds.
3. **He let time do the work.** He didn't try to "time the market" or jump in and out—he just let his investments grow for decades.

Investing isn't about chasing the next big stock. It's about understanding how the game works and playing it wisely. If a gas station attendant with no formal financial education could quietly become a multimillionaire, what's stopping you?

Risk vs. Return - Why Playing It Too Safe Can Be Costly

For decades, financial advisors and cautious investors have followed the same mantra - protect your money. Stick to savings accounts. Keep your wealth in ultra-safe bonds. Avoid the volatility of the stock market. It makes sense, right? After all, no one likes losing money.

But here's the problem - playing it too safe can be just as dangerous as taking on too much risk.

Think about it this way - imagine you bury a chest of gold in your backyard. It feels safe. No market crashes, no economic downturns, no surprises. But fast forward twenty years—while your gold hasn't lost an ounce, the world around it has changed. The price of everything—homes, education, healthcare—has skyrocketed. That same gold chest that once had the power to buy a house might now barely cover a down payment.

This is what happens when you keep all your money in low-risk, low-return investments. Inflation—the silent thief—erodes your purchasing power year after year. And yet, millions of people are still convinced that avoiding risk is the best way to safeguard their future.

The biggest investing mistake isn't buying thc wrong stock. It's not buying any at all.

Consider this - the U.S. stock market has averaged 10% annual returns over the past century. That means if you had invested $10,000 in an index fund tracking the market 30 years ago, you'd now have over $190,000—without lifting a finger.

But here's where fear plays tricks on the mind - short-term drops scare people away. We see headlines screaming about recessions, crashes, and economic slowdowns, and our gut reaction is to pull out. But history shows that long-term patience beats short-term panic every time.

Take the 2008 financial crisis. The stock market dropped nearly 50% in less than two years. Many people sold their investments, convinced the system was broken. Yet, just a decade later, the market had not only recovered but more than tripled. Those who stayed in saw their money multiply. Those who panicked and pulled out locked in their losses forever.

The truth is, the market always experiences downturns—but over the long run, it has consistently grown. Those who stay invested win. Those who sit on the sidelines lose.

Risk isn't one-size-fits-all. Your ability to take financial risks depends on **where you are in life** and how much time you have to recover from downturns.

For young professionals, time is their greatest asset. If a 25-year-old invests in stocks and the market crashes, they still have decades to let it recover. In fact, downturns can even be opportunities—because younger investors can buy more stocks at lower prices, setting them up for even greater long-term gains. But for older investors, the equation changes. If you're 65 and retired, you don't have the luxury of waiting twenty years for the market to bounce back. That's why older investors typically shift towards lower-risk assets like bonds and dividend-paying stocks, ensuring they can withdraw money when they need it without worrying about a sudden market drop.

The Magic of Compounding—Why Time Matters More Than Money

If there's one rule that separates the rich from the poor, it's this - the rich let their money work for them. Most people believe getting wealthy is about earning more. But the truth is, earning more means nothing if you don't invest what you earn.

Imagine two people - Sarah and Tom. Sarah starts investing at age 20, putting just $1,000 into the market. Tom waits until he's 30 to do the same.

By the time they turn 65, assuming a 10% annual return -

- **Sarah's $1,000 grows to $88,000**
- **Tom's $1,000 only grows to $33,000**

Sarah didn't invest more money. She just gave it more time to compound. That's the magic of compounding—your money makes more money, and that money makes even more money.

Imagine rolling a tiny snowball at the top of a mountain. It starts small. But as it moves downhill, it picks up more snow. By the time it reaches the bottom, it's a massive, unstoppable force. That's exactly how compounding works. Your initial investment is small, but as it grows, it starts generating returns. And those returns generate even more returns, creating a cycle that accelerates over time.

The earlier you start, the bigger the snowball. That's why people who start investing in their 20s and 30s almost always end up wealthier than those who start in their 40s and 50s—even if they invest less money overall.

Warren Buffett, one of the world's most successful investors, has a simple rule -

"The stock market is designed to transfer money from the active to the patient."

The smartest investors don't try to predict the market. They just stay in it. Investing small amounts consistently—whether the market is up, down, or sideways—beats trying to jump in and out. If you invest $100 a month every month for 30 years, you'll end up with far more wealth than someone who waits for the "perfect moment" and ends up missing the biggest gains. Because at the end of the day, the biggest driver of wealth isn't money—it's time.

The Investor's Toolkit—How to Build a Simple Portfolio

In 2016, a financial journalist asked Warren Buffett how the average person should invest their money. His response?

"Put 90% in a low-cost S&P 500 index fund and 10% in bonds."

No stock picking. No day trading. No trying to outsmart Wall Street. Just a simple, set-it-and-forget-it approach that's outperformed 90% of professional investors over the past several decades.

Yet, most people make investing far more complicated than it needs to be. They try to pick the next Amazon or Apple, follow "hot stock" tips from the news, or trade based on market predictions—only to end up underperforming a basic index fund. The truth is, the best investors don't chase excitement. They stick to a simple system that works.

If you're looking for the easiest, most effective way to grow wealth without stress, the 3-Fund Portfolio is the answer. It's the closest thing to a "cheat code" in investing. It requires no stock picking, no constant monitoring, and no financial expertise. And yet, it has beaten most actively managed portfolios over time.

Here's how it works -

1. **A Total Stock Market Index Fund** – This gives you broad exposure to the entire stock market. Instead of betting on individual companies, you own a tiny piece of thousands of them. If the stock market grows, so does your investment.
2. **A Bond Fund** – Bonds add stability to your portfolio. They don't grow as fast as stocks, but they also don't crash as hard. When markets are down, bonds help cushion the blow.
3. **An International Fund** – This ensures you're not putting all your eggs in one basket. If the U.S. market underperforms, investments in other countries can keep your portfolio balanced.

That's it. Three funds, covering the entire global economy, with zero effort required.

For most investors, this strategy will outperform 90% of stock pickers. It's not flashy, but it works.

The average investor thinks they need to beat the market to build wealth. They try to find "the next Tesla" or time their trades to maximize profits. But history tells a different story -

- **Even professional investors struggle to pick winning stocks.** In fact, over 90% of actively managed mutual funds fail to beat the market over a 20-year period.
- **Day trading almost always leads to losses.** Studies show that 95% of active traders underperform compared to a simple index fund.

- **Trying to time the market is a losing game.** The best-performing investors aren't the ones who trade the most—they're the ones who leave their money alone.

So why do so many people still try to outsmart the system? Because investing doesn't feel like it should be this easy. We're wired to believe that wealth comes from hard work and complexity—but when it comes to investing, simplicity is the ultimate advantage.

By using a low-cost, diversified portfolio like the 3-Fund Portfolio, you eliminate stress, reduce risk, and let time do the work for you.

The Biggest Investing Myths That Cost People Millions

Investing isn't hard, but people make it harder by believing myths that have been passed down for generations. These misconceptions keep millions of people from ever starting, while others stay trapped in bad strategies that destroy their wealth.

It's time to break those myths once and for all.

Myth #1 - You Need a Lot of Money to Start Investing

For years, people believed that investing was only for the rich—something reserved for Wall Street insiders or those with thousands of dollars to spare.

Reality - You can start investing with as little as $50. Thanks to fractional shares and ETFs (exchange-traded funds), you don't need a fortune to buy stocks. Many brokerage platforms now allow you to invest in a fraction of a share, meaning you can own a piece of companies like Google or Amazon with just a few dollars. Wealth isn't built by having money first. It's built by investing whatever you have—early and consistently.

Myth #2 - The Stock Market is Just Gambling

This might be the most common myth of all. People think investing is like going to a casino—where the house always wins, and regular people lose.

Reality - The market has always grown over time. Yes, stock prices go up and down in the short term. Some days, they drop. Some years, they crash. But over the long run, the market has historically always recovered and reached new highs.

- The Great Depression? Stocks bounced back.
- The 2008 Financial Crisis? The market tripled in the decade after.
- COVID-19? Stocks hit record highs just two years later.

Gambling is random. Investing is based on long-term growth.

Myth #3 - You Should Wait for the "Perfect Time" to Invest

Every time the market drops, people say the same thing - *"I'll wait for stocks to go lower before I invest."*

Reality - Trying to time the market is one of the biggest mistakes you can make.

Research shows that even missing the 10 best days in the stock market over a 30-year period can cut your returns in half. The best strategy? Invest consistently—no matter what the market is doing. Instead of waiting for the perfect moment, set up automatic investments and forget about it. Your future self will thank you.

Myth #4 - Investing is Too Complicated for Beginners

Many people avoid investing because they think they need to be experts. They assume they have to analyze financial reports, track stock movements, and read The Wall Street Journal every morning.

Reality - If you can order coffee online, you can invest. In less than 10 minutes, you can -

- Open a brokerage account
- Buy an index fund
- Set up automatic investments

That's it. No stock picking. No guessing. No complicated strategies. The real secret to investing isn't intelligence—it's consistency.

The most successful investors aren't the ones glued to their screens, analyzing charts, and making trades every day. They're the ones who set their investments on autopilot and forget about them. The best way to ensure you invest consistently? Take willpower out of the equation.

- Set up automatic contributions to your brokerage account.
- Invest a fixed amount every month—whether the market is up or down.
- Let compound interest do the rest.

The more boring your investments, the better they perform. The investors who check their portfolios the least tend to make the most money. The ones who trade the most often end up losing to the market. The more time you spend obsessing over investments, the more likely you are to make bad decisions. The secret to building wealth? Put your money to work—and let time do the rest.

FOR WEALTH GROWTH

Chapter 8 - Investing Beyond the Basics—How to Maximize Growth and Protect Wealth

Dr. Marcus was a man who had mastered control. In the operating room, his hands were steady, his decisions precise. As one of the most sought-after surgeons in his field, he had built his reputation on discipline and meticulous planning. His income reflected his success—half a million dollars a year, enough to buy the life most people dream of. He had the house, the cars, the tailored suits. By every traditional metric, he was a wealthy man.

And yet, when the financial crisis of 2008 hit, he lost nearly everything.

It wasn't because he spent lavishly or lived beyond his means. Dr. Marcus wasn't reckless in the way people usually imagine—he didn't gamble, he didn't burn money on extravagant vacations or make impulsive purchases. His mistake was more subtle, more insidious. He assumed that earning a high income meant he didn't need an investment strategy.

For years, he treated investing as an afterthought. He bought into the hottest tech stocks because his colleagues were doing the same. He put money into real estate without fully understanding how rental income worked. He even backed a few business ventures because they sounded promising, trusting the word of "friends" who assured him of high returns.

Then, the markets collapsed. The stocks he had bought at their peak crumbled overnight. The real estate properties he had bankrolled with little due diligence became financial black holes. The businesses he had funded folded under pressure. Within months, seventy percent of his wealth had vanished.

The irony was brutal. Here was a man who had spent his entire career making high-stakes decisions with confidence, yet when it came to his own money, he had done what so many others do—he had assumed that wealth was a byproduct of income rather than something that needed to be deliberately built, protected, and grown.

Dr. Marcus's story is not unique. It plays out across industries, across professions, across tax brackets. Lottery winners, high-earning professionals, even celebrities—many of them assume that money flows endlessly once it starts coming in. They treat investing as something optional, as something they'll "figure out later." And then, when markets shift, when a crisis hits, when circumstances change, they find themselves scrambling to understand how they ended up in financial ruin.

But there is a reason why some people—not just the already rich, but the quietly wealthy, the long-term investors who build fortunes over decades—never experience this kind of collapse.

It's because they don't rely on income alone. They rely on a system.

The Advanced Investor's Mindset—What Separates the Wealthy from Everyone Else

Most people think of investing as something they "do"—as if it's a singular action, like buying a stock or setting up a retirement account.

They believe the goal is simply to find the right investments, to pick the winners, and to watch their money grow. But the investors who build lasting, generational wealth—the Warren Buffetts, the quiet multimillionaires, the people who remain financially unshaken no matter what happens to the economy—think about investing in an entirely different way.

They don't just invest. They build an investing system. A system means you don't rely on gut feelings or predictions about the market. A system means your investments are protected against downturns. A system means your wealth continues to grow even when you do nothing. This is what separates the advanced investor from the average investor.

The first key difference is how they handle risk. The average investor is driven by emotion—excitement when markets are booming, fear when they crash. When stock prices rise, they invest heavily, assuming the trend will continue. When markets fall, they panic and sell, locking in losses. Their entire strategy is dictated by short-term fluctuations, even though history shows that the biggest returns come to those who stay invested through every cycle.

The wealthy don't operate this way. They prepare for downturns before they happen.

They don't just buy assets expecting them to rise—they position themselves so that even if the market crashes, their wealth remains intact. Some do this by keeping cash reserves, ensuring they have money to invest when prices drop. Others hedge their portfolios with assets that perform well in downturns, like bonds or commodities. The savviest investors even make money when the market crashes by using hedging strategies that protect their wealth from sudden losses.

This is why, while the average investor watches their portfolio shrink in a downturn, wealthy investors are often quietly buying, taking advantage of the discounts while everyone else is selling in fear.

The second key difference is how they use leverage. Most people hear the word "leverage" and think of reckless risk-taking, of overextended debt, of financial ruin. But the wealthy understand that leverage, used correctly, is one of the most powerful tools for compounding wealth.

Take real estate investors. A seasoned real estate investor doesn't simply buy properties with their own cash—they use the bank's money to finance assets that appreciate over time, all while collecting rental income. The return on their actual cash invested is often far greater than if they had bought properties outright.

Stock investors do something similar. They reinvest their dividends, using the market's own returns to compound their wealth faster. Some even use margin loans strategically, borrowing against their investments at low interest rates to acquire more income-producing assets.

But—and this is critical—they never overextend. They only use leverage when the return is greater than the cost of borrowing. They never put themselves in a position where a single market downturn could wipe them out.

The final key difference is their approach to income. Most people invest with the hope that their assets will appreciate over time. They buy stocks, hoping their value will increase. They invest in real estate, expecting property prices to rise. But advanced investors don't just wait for their investments to grow—they make sure their investments pay them right now.

They do this by focusing on passive income. Rather than simply hoping for long-term growth, they invest in assets that generate cash flow. They buy dividend-paying stocks so that they receive payouts even if stock prices stay flat. They invest in real estate not just for appreciation, but for rental income that provides a steady stream of cash. Some go even further, acquiring businesses, royalties, or alternative investments that produce income with minimal effort.

This is what makes wealth bulletproof. When an investor's income is tied to market prices, a downturn can be devastating. But when investments are structured to generate passive income, they continue paying, regardless of what the market is doing. This is why truly wealthy investors remain calm during recessions. While others panic about stock prices falling, they are still collecting rent. They are still receiving dividends. They are still earning passive income from businesses and investments that operate independently of short-term market swings.

The most counterintuitive truth about investing is this - The wealthiest investors aren't the ones chasing the biggest returns. They are the ones who have created a system where their money works for them no matter what.

And this is where Dr. Marcus failed.

He had the income. He had the knowledge. But he didn't have the system. He treated investing like a collection of random decisions rather than a structured plan. And when the market shifted, he had nothing protecting him. The true secret of the world's most successful investors isn't that they're smarter than everyone else. It's that they build frameworks that remove emotion, maximize efficiency, and ensure that they always have money working for them.

The Art of Protecting Wealth—Why Defense Matters as Much as Offense

There's a dangerous illusion in investing—the belief that wealth-building is all about offense. People chase returns, trying to maximize their gains, convinced that the only thing that matters is how much their portfolio grows. But the most sophisticated investors, the ones who stay wealthy for decades, know that defense matters just as much as offense.

Because in investing, it's not just what you make—it's what you keep. History is littered with examples of brilliant investors who made millions, only to lose everything because they ignored risk. They weren't reckless gamblers or naive beginners. They were people who had spent years accumulating wealth, only to be wiped out in a moment because they failed to do one thing - protect what they had already built.

Why does this happen? Overconfidence. Many investors, after years of success, start believing they are untouchable. They assume they can predict markets. They take on too much risk, thinking they've figured out a formula for never losing. And then, when an inevitable downturn comes, they're completely unprepared. This is why some of the greatest investors in history—including billionaires, hedge fund managers, and financial institutions—have lost staggering amounts of money. They underestimated three critical risks that can wipe out years of gains in an instant.

Market Crashes - The Unavoidable Test of Every Investor

Every bull market creates a sense of invincibility. People assume stocks will keep going up, that real estate will never crash, that their investments are fundamentally safe. Then, without warning, everything collapses.

The 2008 financial crisis erased $10 trillion in global stock market value in a matter of months. The 2000 dot-com crash wiped out entire fortunes overnight. The COVID-19 pandemic sent markets spiraling in ways no one expected. And yet, every time, the same thing happens - investors who assumed “this time is different” get wiped out. So, how do you protect yourself? By structuring your portfolio to survive economic downturns before they happen.

Smart investors don’t just invest for the good times. They prepare for the bad ones.

That means having a diversified portfolio—not just stocks, but assets that tend to perform well when markets crash. It means keeping enough cash reserves so that you’re never forced to sell assets at the worst possible time. It means resisting the urge to go all-in on any one investment, no matter how promising it seems.

Most importantly, it means understanding that market cycles are inevitable. If you invest expecting every year to be a winning year, you will fail. The ones who stay wealthy are the ones who plan for the crashes before they come.

Sequence of Returns Risk - The Hidden Trap for Retirees

Imagine two people retire with the same amount of money—one in 1995 and one in 2000. They both withdraw the same percentage of their portfolio every year. But one of them lives comfortably in retirement while the other runs out of money. How is that possible? Because when you withdraw matters as much as how much you withdraw.

This is called sequence of returns risk. If you retire during a bull market, your portfolio grows even as you make withdrawals. But if you retire at the start of a bear market, you're withdrawing from a shrinking portfolio, which accelerates your losses.

The solution? The bucket strategy.

Instead of relying solely on investments that fluctuate with the market, smart retirees keep short-term cash reserves that allow them to avoid selling stocks in a downturn. They divide their portfolio into three "buckets" -

1. **Cash and short-term bonds** for immediate withdrawals (1-3 years).
2. **Dividend-paying stocks and conservative investments** for medium-term needs (4-10 years).
3. **Long-term growth assets** that they don't touch unless absolutely necessary (10+ years).

This ensures that when markets crash, they aren't forced to sell at a loss.

The Wealth Multiplier—Using Smart Leverage Without Risking It All

The rich get richer not because they invest differently—but because they use money differently. The average investor thinks in terms of cash. They invest whatever they've saved. When they run out of savings, they stop investing. But the wealthy think in terms of leverage. They don't just invest their own money—they use borrowed money strategically to amplify returns, without taking reckless risks. The key is knowing the difference between good debt and bad debt.

Good Debt vs. Bad Debt - The Rules of Smart Borrowing

Not all debt is bad. In fact, some of the wealthiest investors use debt to build fortunes. But they do it in a way that never puts them in a position to lose everything. Bad debt is debt that drains wealth—credit card debt, payday loans, high-interest personal loans. It funds things that lose value. Good debt is debt that builds wealth—real estate loans, business loans, margin loans that allow you to invest at low interest rates. The key is that it must always be backed by an asset that appreciates or generates income.

The classic example of smart leverage is real estate. Most real estate investors don't pay for properties in cash. They use the bank's money. They put down 20%, borrow the rest, and then use rental income to cover the mortgage. Over time, as property values rise and the mortgage gets paid down, they build wealth using money they never had to save themselves. They never overleverage. They ensure their rental income more than covers their mortgage and expenses, so they never have to pay out of pocket.

Some investors take leverage even further by borrowing against their stock portfolio using margin loans. The logic is simple - If you can borrow at 3% interest and invest in assets that earn 8-10%, you pocket the difference. But there's a risk. Unlike real estate loans, which are stable, margin loans can be called in at any time. If your investments drop in value, the brokerage can demand you pay back the loan immediately, forcing you to sell at a loss. This is why only advanced investors use margin—and only when they have enough cash reserves to cover a sudden downturn.

Many homeowners sit on massive equity without realizing they can use it as an investment tool. Home Equity Lines of Credit (HELOCs) allow you to borrow against your home's value at much lower interest rates than personal loans or credit cards. The key is using this debt to invest in income-producing assets, not lifestyle expenses. The One Rule That Protects You From Disaster

The difference between smart leverage and reckless leverage comes down to one critical rule - *Never take on debt without a clear exit strategy.*

The people who get into trouble with leverage aren't the ones who borrow—it's the ones who borrow without knowing how they'll pay it back. This is why wealthy investors always have contingencies. They stress-test their finances, ensuring that even if the market crashes, they can still cover their debts. Used correctly, leverage is the ultimate wealth multiplier. Used recklessly, it's a financial time bomb. And understanding this difference is what separates those who build wealth from those who lose it.

The Passive Income Playbook—How to Turn Investments Into Cash Flow

If there's one thing the wealthy understand that most investors overlook, it's this - money should work for you, not the other way around. Most people focus on growing their net worth—watching their portfolio value rise, checking their account balances, celebrating when stocks go up. But what good is having millions on paper if it doesn't translate into real, usable income? This is where the true power of passive income comes in.

Passive income isn't about making quick money. It's about structuring your investments so that cash flows into your account consistently—without you having to sell assets or actively manage them. The wealthy don't just invest for capital appreciation. They invest in a way that pays them regularly, so their money works for them even while they sleep.

There are three major ways to generate passive investment income -

Dividend Stocks & ETFs—Getting Paid Just for Owning Shares

Imagine a company that not only grows in value but also pays you every few months just for owning a piece of it. That's exactly what dividend stocks do. When a company earns profits, it has two choices - reinvest that money into growing the business or distribute some of it back to shareholders in the form of dividends. The best companies do both—they grow, and they reward investors along the way.

Take Coca-Cola. If you had invested in Coca-Cola stock 30 years ago, not only would your shares be worth significantly more today, but you'd also be earning a steady stream of income from dividends. In fact, some long-term investors who bought decades ago earn more in annual dividends than they originally paid for their shares. For those who don't want to research individual companies, dividend ETFs make passive income even easier. These funds hold dozens or hundreds of dividend-paying stocks, ensuring a steady stream of cash without the risk of betting on a single company.

Avoid the temptation to chase high yields. Some companies offer extremely high dividends, but that often signals trouble. If a stock is paying 10% or more in dividends, it might not be sustainable. Many investors fall into this trap, only to watch their dividends disappear when the company runs into trouble.

The safest way to invest in dividend stocks is to focus on consistency, not just high payouts. Look for companies with a long history of increasing dividends—these businesses tend to survive recessions and market downturns while still rewarding investors.

Rental Properties & REITs—The Real Estate Cash Machine

Real estate is one of the oldest and most powerful forms of passive income investing. It's how ordinary people build generational wealth—not just through rising property values but through monthly rental income that pays the bills.

The core strategy is simple - Buy a property that generates more rent than it costs to own.

This is how real estate investors build wealth with other people's money. They use the bank's money (a mortgage) to buy an asset, then let renters pay the mortgage for them. Over time, rents go up, the mortgage gets paid down, and the investor ends up with a property that provides steady cash flow for life. However, rental real estate isn't for everyone. Tenants can be a headache, maintenance costs add up, and managing properties takes time.

For those who want the benefits of real estate investing without the hassle, there's a simpler alternative - Real Estate Investment Trusts (REITs). REITs are companies that own and manage income-generating properties, from apartment buildings to office spaces to shopping centers. Instead of buying a rental property yourself, you can buy shares of a REIT—which means you still earn passive rental income, but without the stress of dealing with tenants.

Selling Covered Calls & Options Income

For investors who already own stocks, there's a way to generate even more income from them—without selling. This strategy is called selling covered calls. It's a technique that lets you collect cash from traders who are willing to pay you for the right to buy your shares.

Here's how it works. Let's say you own 100 shares of Apple. Instead of just holding onto them, you sell a covered call, which is essentially an agreement saying -

"If Apple's price reaches a certain level within the next month, I'll sell my shares to you at that price. But in exchange, you have to pay me now—whether the stock hits that level or not."

If Apple never reaches that price, you keep your stock and the money you were paid upfront. If it does, you still make a profit from selling at a predetermined price.

Sophisticated investors use this strategy to generate consistent cash flow from stocks they already own, without taking on significant risk.

The Smart Investor's Tax Strategy—Keeping More of What You Earn

Most investors focus on how much they make. The smartest investors focus on how much they keep. The tax system isn't designed to punish the rich. It's designed to reward people who understand how to play by the rules. The wealthy don't pay lower tax rates because they cheat the system. They pay lower rates because they use the system to their advantage. There are three key tax advantages that advanced investors use to legally minimize what they owe.

1. Tax-Efficient Asset Placement

Not all investments should be held in the same type of account. For example, growth stocks belong in Roth accounts—because you won't owe taxes when they appreciate. Bonds should be in tax-deferred accounts—because interest income is taxed at high rates. High-dividend stocks should stay in taxable accounts—because they get special lower tax rates. By simply placing investments in the right accounts, you can save thousands in taxes over time—without changing your portfolio.

2. Capital Gains Tax Strategies

Most people don't realize this, but long-term capital gains are taxed at much lower rates than regular income. If you hold an investment for more than a year, the tax rate on your gains drops dramatically. And in some cases, it's 0%. For example, in the U.S., if your taxable income is under a certain threshold, you pay no taxes at all on long-term capital gains. Even for higher earners, capital gains are still taxed at lower rates than ordinary income—so long-term investing is not just smart for wealth-building, it's smart for tax savings.

Here's another strategy - tax-loss harvesting. If you have an investment that's down, you can sell it, take the loss, and use it to offset gains elsewhere—reducing your tax bill.

3. The 1031 Exchange

For real estate investors, there's one tax strategy that allows them to buy and sell properties without ever paying capital gains tax. It's called a 1031 exchange.

Here's how it works. When you sell a rental property, instead of paying taxes on your profit, you reinvest that money into a new property. By doing this, your tax bill gets deferred indefinitely. This is why some real estate investors never pay capital gains tax for their entire lives. They just keep rolling their profits into bigger and better properties, compounding their wealth tax-free.

The Final Investing Level

Money, for most people, is about security. It's about paying bills, covering unexpected expenses, and maybe even splurging on a vacation. But for those who understand how to use investing to its fullest potential, money is about something far greater—freedom.

Financial freedom is the point where you no longer work for money; your investments work for you. It's waking up every morning knowing that your bills are covered, your future is secure, and whether you choose to work or not, your lifestyle remains unchanged. This isn't about being a billionaire. You don't need private jets or sprawling mansions. True financial freedom is reaching a point where your investment income fully replaces your expenses—so work becomes optional.

Most people never get there because they either -

1. Assume they need **tens of millions** to retire.
2. Invest without a clear strategy, hoping their money "somehow" lasts.
3. Underestimate how long their savings can sustain them.

If you invest wisely, you can reach financial independence far sooner than you think. The key is understanding how to structure your portfolio to generate reliable income without running out of money. Let's break down the strategies that make it possible.

The 4% Rule—How to Live Off Your Portfolio Forever

One of the most powerful and widely studied financial principles is the 4% rule—a research-backed method that determines how much you can safely withdraw from your investments each year without ever running out of money.

The concept is simple. If you withdraw 4% of your portfolio annually (adjusted for inflation), there's a very high probability your money will last 30+ years—even in bad markets. This means that for every $1 million in investments, you can safely withdraw $40,000 per year without worrying about going broke. If you need $80,000 a year to live comfortably, you'll need around $2 million saved.

This rule works because even with market downturns, a well-diversified portfolio of stocks and bonds typically earns 6–8% per year on average over long periods. If you're only withdrawing 4%, your money grows enough to replenish itself—even as you spend it.

Most people don't believe this works. Many investors fear taking money out, convinced that if the market crashes, they'll lose everything. But the 4% rule isn't based on hope—it's based on decades of historical data, tested through crashes, recessions, and economic turmoil.

Here's a real-world example. If you had retired in 1973—right before the worst bear market in decades—your portfolio would have still lasted 30+ years following the 4% rule. If you retired in 2000, just before the dot-com bubble burst, you'd still be fine. Even through 2008's financial crisis, this strategy survived. Of course, no system is foolproof. That's why flexibility matters. If markets take a nosedive, temporarily lowering withdrawals from 4% to 3% in a bad year can help your portfolio recover.

The biggest mistake? Not trusting the math. Investors who panic and pull all their money into cash when the market drops end up locked out of the recovery—and ironically, this increases their risk of running out of money.

A structured withdrawal plan, backed by historical data, is the safest way to turn investments into a lifetime income stream.

The Barbell Approach—Balancing Safety and Growth

One of the greatest fears retirees face is losing money in a market crash right after they stop working. It's a real risk—if you withdraw from your portfolio during a downturn, you're pulling out money before your investments have a chance to recover. That's where the barbell strategy comes in.

The idea is simple. Instead of putting all your money into stocks (which can be volatile) or all your money into cash (which loses value to inflation), you balance between both. You keep 2–3 years' worth of living expenses in cash or ultra-safe bonds—so if a market crash happens, you're not forced to sell stocks at a loss. Meanwhile, the rest of your portfolio remains fully invested—ensuring long-term growth. This strategy acts as a psychological buffer. Knowing you have cash on hand prevents panic-selling when the market drops—allowing you to ride out volatility without making emotional mistakes.

Here's what it looks like in practice. If you need $60,000 per year to live on, keep $120,000–$180,000 in cash or short-term bonds. If the market drops, use this reserve instead of selling stocks at a loss. When the market recovers, refill your cash buffer by selling investments at a profit. This system ensures you never withdraw from your portfolio at the worst possible time.

Most investors do the opposite - they panic, sell everything in a downturn, then wait too long to reinvest. The barbell strategy prevents this cycle—protecting your money while allowing for growth.

The Bridge Strategy—Covering Early Retirement Before Social Security Kicks In

One of the biggest gaps in retirement planning is the "early retirement phase." Many investors want to retire in their 50s, but Social Security and pension benefits often don't start until their 60s. This creates a 5–10-year gap where they need income—but don't want to drain their investments too quickly.

Enter the bridge strategy. The goal is to set aside specific funds that cover the early years of retirement—so you don't have to touch your long-term investment accounts prematurely.

Here's how it works. Save extra cash or conservative investments in a separate "bridge" fund—enough to cover expenses for 5–10 years. Use this money first before withdrawing from retirement accounts. By the time Social Security (or pensions) kick in, your main investment portfolio has had more time to grow—reducing the total amount you need to withdraw.

This approach works especially well for people retiring in their 50s or early 60s.

Let's say you plan to retire at 55 and need $50,000 per year to live on. If you've built up $300,000 in a separate bridge fund, you can cover six years of living expenses without touching your main portfolio. By age 61, your retirement investments have had six extra years to grow—and you can start withdrawing at a much safer rate.

This strategy prevents early withdrawals from tax-advantaged accounts, helps minimize taxes, and provides a psychological cushion—you won't feel pressured to start selling investments too soon.

Winning the Investing Game - When Work Becomes Optional

Reaching financial freedom doesn't happen by accident. It requires strategy, patience, and the right mindset. Too many people assume investing is about hitting a magic number—"I need $5 million to retire." But the reality is, financial independence isn't just about how much you have—it's about how your investments are structured.

If you have passive income streams from dividends, real estate, and strategic withdrawals, you don't need tens of millions to live comfortably. If you structure your portfolio correctly, your money can last forever—without you ever having to work again. If you understand risk, taxes, and market cycles, you won't fall into the same traps that cause even high earners to lose everything.

The final level of investing isn't about chasing the highest returns—it's about structuring your wealth in a way that guarantees you never run out of money.

Because, in the end, the real goal isn't money.

It's freedom.

The difference between people who struggle with money and those who build wealth isn't intelligence. It's action. You don't need to be perfect. You don't need to have all the answers. But you do need to start. So here's your challenge: automate one small financial decision today. Whether it's setting up a savings transfer, increasing your 401(k) contribution, or canceling a wasteful subscription—just start. Because every day you wait is a day wealth-building opportunities slip away.

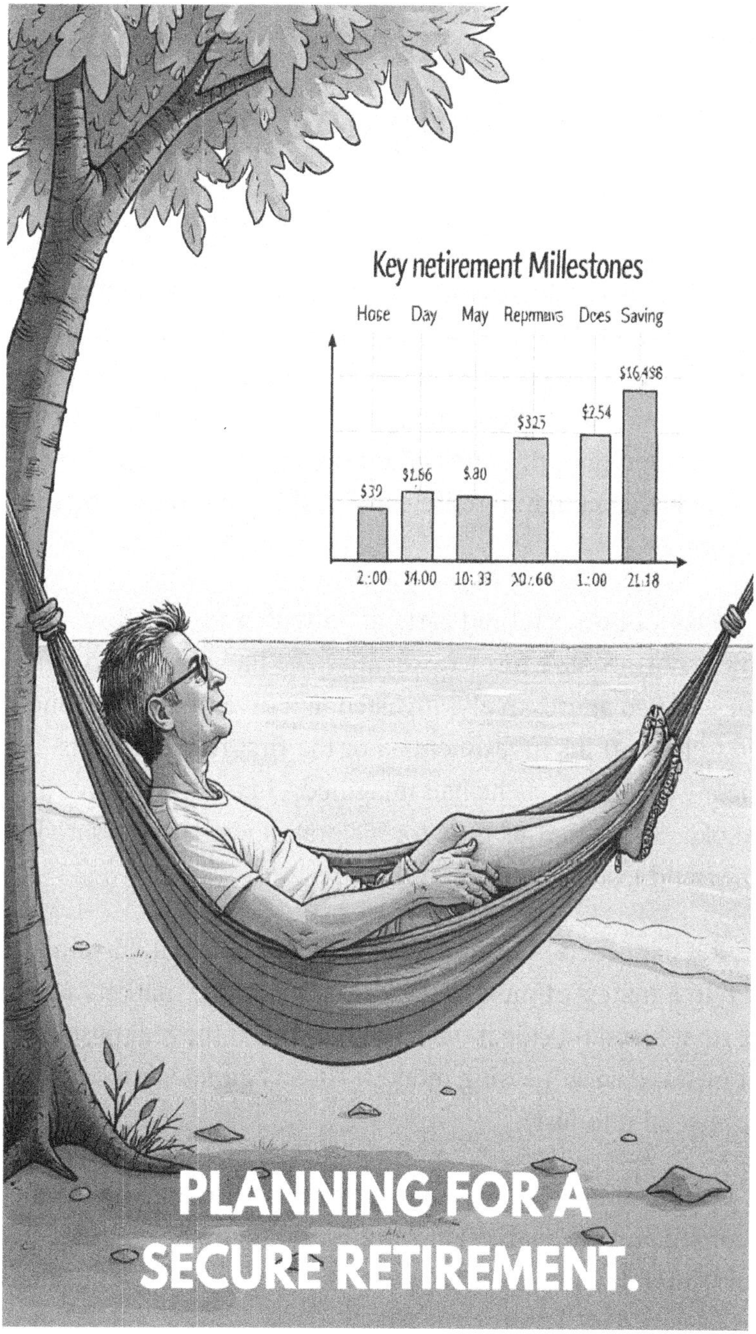
Key netirement Millestones
Hose Day May Dces Saving
$39
$1.66
$.80
$325
$2.54
$16,458
2::00 14:00 10:33 1::00 21:18
PLANNING FOR A SECURE RETIREMENT.

Chapter 9 - Retirement Planning—The Real Endgame of Wealth

Nearly 50% of Canadians are at risk of running out of money in retirement. In the U.S., the average retiree has just $95,776 in savings—far below what's needed for a comfortable life. And yet, most people don't think about retirement until it's too late. Retirement isn't just about stopping work—it's about financial freedom. The question is: will you have enough to retire comfortably, or will you be forced to keep working?

In 1997, Daniel Foster retired early at 55 with a $1.2 million investment portfolio. A former executive, he had done everything by the book—saved aggressively, invested in a diversified portfolio, and planned to live off his investments. For the first few years, his retirement was exactly as he had imagined - luxury vacations, a cottage in Muskoka, and generous gifts for his grandkids. He was sure his savings would last him the rest of his life.

Then, 2008 happened. The financial crisis wiped out 40% of his portfolio in a matter of months. He told himself the markets would recover, that he could ride it out. But that wasn't the real problem. His biggest mistake wasn't losing money—it was underestimating how long he'd need it to last.

By 75, Daniel realized he was in trouble. Withdrawing too much too early, combined with market downturns and rising healthcare costs, had left him with a dwindling nest egg. His CPP payments weren't nearly enough, and without a pension, he had no safety net. His final option? Going back to work at 78—not because he wanted to, but because he had no other choice.

Daniel's story highlights a brutal truth about retirement - it's not just about saving—it's about ensuring your money outlasts you. Many people believe they'll be fine as long as they hit some arbitrary "magic number," but the reality is far more complex. Retirement isn't about reaching a specific savings target—it's about creating a sustainable, resilient financial plan that accounts for market crashes, rising costs, and the biggest unknown of all—how long you'll live.

How Much Do You Really Need?

Walk into any financial planner's office, and you'll hear the same question - "How much do I need to retire?" Some will tell you $1 million, others $2 million, or even $5 million. But the real answer? It depends. There is no universal "magic number" that guarantees a comfortable retirement. Instead, the right amount depends on three critical factors -

1. **Your Spending, Not Just Your Savings**

Too many people focus on the size of their nest egg without asking the more important question - How much will you spend in retirement?

- A retiree who needs $40,000 per year to live can retire with far less than someone who needs $100,000 per year.
- The mistake most people make? Assuming expenses will drop significantly in retirement. While some costs—like commuting or work clothes—may go away, others (healthcare, travel, home maintenance) often increase.

A better way to plan is backward - Instead of focusing on a savings goal, calculate your annual spending needs first. Then, determine how much you'll need to generate that level of income sustainably.

2. The Length of Your Retirement

Most people assume they'll live into their 80s. But what if you live to 95 or even 100?

- Retiring at 55 means funding 35-40 years of expenses.
- Retiring at 70 may require only 20 years of savings.
- Life expectancy is increasing, but most retirement plans don't account for unexpected longevity risk—outliving your money.

The financial industry calls this "longevity risk," but a better term might be "the nightmare of running out of money." This is why most financial planners now recommend planning for a 30+ year retirement, even if you retire later in life.

3. The Sustainability of Your Income Streams

Not all retirement savings are created equal. Two retirees with $1 million saved may have completely different levels of financial security, depending on where that money is held and invested.

- **Retiree A** - Invests mostly in the stock market—potentially high returns, but vulnerable to market crashes.
- **Retiree B** - Has a mix of rental properties, dividend stocks, and a pension—a more stable, diversified income.

The key difference? Sustainability. If the market crashes, Retiree A might be forced to sell assets at a loss. Retiree B, on the other hand, can rely on other income sources to wait out a downturn.

The best retirement plans aren't just about how much you save—they're about how you structure your income to be stable, diversified, and resilient to market fluctuations.

The Real Retirement Safety Net—What They Offer (And What They Don't)

For decades, people have been told that government pensions will take care of them in retirement. The idea was simple - work for 40 years, contribute to the system, and enjoy a steady check in old age. But the reality today is far more complicated. The safety net is there, but it is riddled with holes. For many, it catches just enough to prevent outright financial disaster—but not enough to provide real security. Those who rely on government programs alone often find themselves trapped in a cycle of just getting by rather than enjoying the retirement they envisioned.

In Canada, the Canada Pension Plan (CPP) was designed as a supplement, not a full retirement plan. Yet many Canadians assume it will be enough. The maximum monthly CPP payout sits at $1,364, but here's the catch—most people don't get the maximum. The average payout is closer to $770 a month. That's less than minimum wage in most provinces. Old Age Security (OAS), which adds another layer of support, provides up to $707 per month, but it comes with a built-in trap - if you earn too much in retirement, the government starts clawing it back. And for those in real financial need, the Guaranteed Income Supplement (GIS) can help, but only if you earn next to nothing from other sources. The system rewards those with little to no savings while penalizing those who did just well enough to cross the income thresholds.

The situation in the United States is just as precarious. Social Security was never meant to be a retiree's primary income—it was designed as a last resort, a safety net to catch those who had no other means of support. Yet today, millions of Americans depend on it as their main source of income. On average, Social Security replaces just 40% of a worker's pre-retirement income. For most retirees, that's a dramatic pay cut. If you claim early at 62, your monthly benefit is reduced for life. If you wait until full retirement age (67), you get more—but still not enough to maintain the standard of living most people expect. And while Medicare covers healthcare costs, it does not cover long-term care, one of the biggest financial burdens in old age. Nursing homes and assisted living facilities can wipe out a lifetime of savings in just a few years.

The biggest mistake retirees make is assuming these government programs will be enough. They won't. Social Security, CPP, and OAS are designed to keep retirees from falling into poverty, not to provide a comfortable lifestyle. A single senior relying solely on these programs in Canada will likely have an income below $25,000 per year. In the U.S., the numbers are similar. Without other income sources, retirement becomes a constant battle to stretch every dollar, with little room for travel, hobbies, or even unexpected medical expenses.

This is where the harsh truth emerges - government benefits should be treated as a bonus, not a retirement plan. If you structure your finances assuming CPP or Social Security will cover everything, you are setting yourself up for disappointment. Instead, these payments should be viewed as just one piece of a broader retirement strategy—an extra cushion, not the foundation. The real safety net is the one you build yourself through savings, investments, and alternative income streams.

How to Build a Sustainable Retirement Income

Saving money is only half the equation in retirement planning. The real challenge is turning that money into a steady, sustainable income that lasts for the rest of your life. Many people assume that once they've saved enough, they can simply withdraw from their nest egg as needed.

But this approach is dangerously flawed. Without a clear strategy for withdrawals, tax efficiency, and diversification, retirees can find themselves running out of money far sooner than expected.

The best retirement income plans are built on multiple streams of cash flow. The traditional model—drawing down from an RRSP or 401(k) and hoping it lasts—is no longer enough. A modern retirement portfolio needs to include a mix of investments, dividends, real estate, and possibly even passive income sources that allow for flexibility. The key is designing a system where income is generated without depleting principal too quickly.

Investment withdrawals from registered accounts form the backbone of most retirement strategies. In Canada, this means tapping into RRSPs, which convert into Registered Retirement Income Funds (RRIFs) at age 71, requiring minimum withdrawals each year. In the U.S., 401(k)s and IRAs serve a similar function, with required minimum distributions (RMDs) kicking in at 73.

The challenge with these accounts is taxation—every withdrawal is taxed as regular income, which can push retirees into higher tax brackets if they withdraw too much at once. This is why tax-free accounts like the TFSA in Canada or the Roth IRA in the U.S. play a critical role. Money withdrawn from these accounts is not taxed, making them ideal for supplementing income without increasing taxable earnings.

Beyond traditional investment accounts, dividends provide one of the best ways to create consistent, passive income. A portfolio of dividend-paying stocks or ETFs can generate cash flow without the need to sell off assets.

The advantage here is twofold - first, retirees continue earning money even during market downturns, reducing the need to sell investments at a loss. Second, high-quality dividend stocks often increase their payouts over time, creating an income stream that keeps up with inflation. However, many investors make the mistake of chasing high-yield stocks without considering risk. A 10% dividend yield might look attractive, but if the underlying company is struggling, those payments may not last. The smarter approach is to focus on companies with a strong history of dividend growth and financial stability.

For those looking beyond the stock market, real estate remains one of the most powerful tools for building retirement income. Owning rental properties provides a hedge against inflation, as rents tend to rise over time. But being a landlord is not for everyone. Property management, tenant issues, and unexpected repairs can turn real estate into a second job rather than a passive investment. For retirees who want real estate exposure without the headaches, Real Estate Investment Trusts (REITs) offer an alternative. These publicly traded companies own and operate income-generating properties, from apartment buildings to shopping centers, and distribute rental income to investors in the form of dividends. This allows retirees to benefit from real estate appreciation and cash flow without dealing with direct ownership.

For those who prefer guaranteed income, pensions and annuities offer a level of security that few other investments can match. Defined benefit pensions, which provide a set payout for life, have become increasingly rare outside of government and union jobs. For those without a pension, annuities can fill the gap. By converting a lump sum into regular payments, annuities provide steady income that lasts a lifetime. But they come with drawbacks—high fees, limited flexibility, and the risk of locking up money that could be better invested elsewhere. While annuities can serve a role in a diversified retirement plan, they should be approached carefully, with an understanding of the trade-offs involved.

The most effective retirement portfolios balance security with growth. Too much exposure to bonds and cash leaves retirees vulnerable to inflation, while an overreliance on stocks increases the risk of major losses in a market downturn. A structured approach, often called the barbell strategy, provides a way to navigate these risks.

On one end of the barbell, retirees hold stable, guaranteed income sources—CPP, OAS, Social Security, pensions, or annuities. On the other end, they maintain growth assets—stocks, ETFs, and real estate—to ensure their portfolio keeps pace with inflation. In the middle, they keep liquid assets like cash and short-term bonds to serve as a buffer during market downturns. This strategy ensures retirees always have access to funds without being forced to sell investments at a loss.

The mistake most retirees make isn't failing to save—it's failing to plan for how to turn savings into income. Without a clear withdrawal strategy, retirees either deplete their funds too quickly or live so frugally that they never truly enjoy their retirement years. The key is balance—using a mix of registered accounts, dividend income, real estate, and pensions to create a system that provides stability without sacrificing growth. The best retirement plans aren't just about having enough money. They're about structuring that money in a way that guarantees it lasts a lifetime.

How to Fund Your Retirement Accounts

Most people assume that simply opening an RRSP, TFSA, or 401(k) is enough. They set up an account, contribute sporadically when they remember, and hope that somehow, by the time they retire, the money will be there. But retirement accounts don't grow by magic—they grow because of consistent, strategic funding, and the people who retire wealthy understand that *how* you contribute is just as important as *where* you invest.

The biggest myth about funding retirement is that you need huge lump sums to make a difference. The truth is, small, consistent contributions—automated and strategically placed—build fortunes over decades. The $500 you automatically contribute every month to a TFSA or 401(k) today might feel insignificant, but compounded over 30 years, it turns into hundreds of thousands of dollars. The problem is, most people don't start early enough, don't invest aggressively enough, or don't take full advantage of the accounts available to them.

The first step to properly funding your retirement accounts is treating it like a non-negotiable expense. Just like your rent or mortgage gets paid every month, your future financial security should be prioritized the same way. If your employer offers a Group RRSP, 401(k), or DPSP with matching contributions, maxing that out should be your first move—not just because it's an easy way to save, but because it's free money. If your employer is willing to match 5% of your salary and you're not taking advantage, you're literally leaving money on the table. A person earning $80,000 who contributes 5% annually gets an additional $4,000 a year from their employer. Over a 30-year career, that's $120,000 in free money—and that's before any investment growth.

Beyond employer plans, maximizing tax-advantaged accounts is the second pillar of funding retirement. In Canada, that means prioritizing your TFSA and RRSP, while in the U.S., it means Roth IRAs and traditional IRAs in addition to your 401(k). TFSAs and Roth IRAs are especially powerful because withdrawals are tax-free, meaning the government never touches that money again. Contributing the maximum annually ensures that every dollar you invest has the longest time to grow tax-free.

A smart funding strategy also involves optimizing tax deductions. RRSP contributions in Canada and 401(k) contributions in the U.S. reduce taxable income, which means they don't just help your future self—they also reduce the taxes you pay today. The wealthy take full advantage of this, using RRSP contributions to drop themselves into lower tax brackets, saving thousands of dollars each year that can be reinvested.

The most overlooked way to fund retirement accounts is redirecting raises, bonuses, and windfalls. Most people, when they get a raise, expand their lifestyle—they move into a bigger house, lease a more expensive car, or take a luxury vacation. But those who retire wealthy increase their savings rate instead. If you receive a 5% raise, rather than increasing your spending, direct that additional income into your RRSP or TFSA before you even see it. This is how wealth is built—not by earning more, but by ensuring that as income grows, *savings grow alongside it.*

The Silent Wealth Killer—Why Inflation Destroys Retirements

In 1970, a cup of coffee cost 25 cents. Today, that same cup in a diner will cost anywhere between $3 and $5, depending on where you live. A loaf of bread that was once 30 cents is now over $3. Inflation isn't something that hits all at once like a market crash—it's a slow, creeping erosion of purchasing power that most people don't notice until it's too late. The biggest mistake retirees make is assuming that their money today will hold the same value 10, 20, or 30 years into the future. It won't.

Inflation is the silent killer of wealth, and yet, most retirement plans fail to account for its impact. Even at what seems like a modest 2% annual inflation rate, the cost of living doubles roughly every 36 years. That means someone retiring at 65 with $1 million in savings will effectively have just $500,000 worth of purchasing power by the time they're 101. And that's assuming inflation stays low—history has shown that during certain periods, it spikes dramatically. In the 1970s, inflation hit double digits, wiping out the savings of those who had planned for a much lower cost of living. A retirement plan that looks sufficient today can quickly become inadequate if inflation outpaces expectations.

The people who suffer the most from inflation are those on fixed incomes. Many retirees assume they can live off their savings or pension for decades, only to find that the cost of everything—groceries, healthcare, property taxes—steadily rises while their income stays the same. A pension that seemed generous at $3,000 per month in 1990 would now feel painfully insufficient. Government benefits like CPP and Social Security adjust for inflation, but not nearly enough to keep pace with rising expenses. This is why retirees who assume they've saved "enough" often find themselves cutting corners and scaling back their lifestyles as time goes on.

The biggest myth about retirement planning is that being conservative with investments is the safest approach. In reality, keeping everything in low-risk, low-return assets like bonds or GICs can be one of the riskiest moves. While these investments provide stability, they fail to grow fast enough to outpace inflation. That's why retirees need to maintain exposure to assets that grow over time. Stocks, for instance, remain one of the best defenses against inflation. Over long periods, the stock market has consistently outperformed inflation, ensuring that a portion of a retiree's portfolio continues to grow. Dividend-paying stocks, in particular, provide a hedge, as many companies increase their payouts over time, keeping up with rising costs.

Real estate offers another powerful protection against inflation. Property values and rental income tend to rise alongside inflation, meaning that retirees who own real estate can maintain their purchasing power even as the cost of living increases. A rental property that generates $1,500 per month in rent today may produce $2,500 a decade from now, keeping pace with rising expenses. Even those who don't want the hassle of being landlords can invest in REITs, which provide exposure to real estate without the hands-on management.

Inflation is inevitable, but financial ruin in retirement is not. The key is to ensure that a portion of your wealth is in assets that will continue to grow, rather than simply trying to preserve what you have. Retirement is not just about having a big enough nest egg on day one—it's about making sure that nest egg keeps up with the real cost of living over time.

The Withdrawal Problem—How to Make Your Money Last

Imagine two retirees, both starting with $1 million in savings. They each plan to withdraw $50,000 per year to cover their expenses. The only difference between them is timing. Retiree A enters retirement during a bull market. His investments continue to grow, even as he makes withdrawals. By the time he's 80, his portfolio has actually increased in value despite years of spending. Retiree B, on the other hand, retires right before a market crash. His $1 million drops to $700,000 within the first two years, and as he continues withdrawing money to cover his expenses, his portfolio shrinks even further. By the time he's 80, he's running out of money.

This is the sequence of returns risk, one of the most dangerous yet overlooked threats in retirement planning. It's not just how much you withdraw that determines whether your money lasts—it's when you withdraw it in relation to market performance. Retiring into a bear market can be financially catastrophic if you're forced to sell investments at a loss to generate cash.

The traditional 4% rule—where you withdraw 4% of your portfolio annually—works under the assumption of stable market returns. But in reality, markets don't move in straight lines. A few bad years early in retirement can throw an entire plan off course. This is why the best retirement strategies include buffer assets—liquid funds that can cover expenses when markets are down, so you don't have to sell investments at the worst possible time.

One of the simplest ways to mitigate sequence risk is to keep two to three years' worth of expenses in cash or short-term bonds. This acts as a cushion during downturns, allowing retirees to ride out market volatility without depleting their principal. Another strategy is to adjust withdrawals based on market conditions. In strong years, taking a bit more is fine. In weak years, pulling back spending can significantly extend the lifespan of a portfolio.

For those who want absolute security, annuities or pensions can provide guaranteed income, eliminating the worry of market fluctuations altogether. The trade-off, of course, is flexibility—once money is converted into an annuity, it's locked in. But for retirees who value stability over upside potential, having a portion of their income guaranteed can provide peace of mind.

The biggest mistake retirees make isn't spending too much—it's not having a strategy for how to withdraw money in a way that ensures it lasts. Retirement isn't just about building wealth. It's about managing it intelligently so that it supports you for the rest of your life.

How to Retire on Your Terms

At its core, retirement isn't about stopping work. It's about **having the freedom to choose** what to do with your time. The happiest retirees aren't necessarily the wealthiest—they're the ones who remain engaged, whether through work, hobbies, travel, or community involvement. Retirement is often portrayed as an endless vacation, but the reality is that most people don't want to sit on a beach for 30 years. The people who thrive in retirement are those who **have a purpose** beyond just financial security.

Some choose to keep working—not because they have to, but because they enjoy it. A retiree who spent decades in a high-stress corporate job might pivot to part-time consulting or teaching. Others dive into passion projects, volunteering, or starting small businesses. The key difference between a good retirement and a great one is choice. The more financial flexibility you have, the more control you have over how you spend your time.

For those who dream of travel, hobbies, or new experiences, the financial foundation laid today determines what's possible in the future. A well-structured retirement plan is what allows someone to say yes—to a spontaneous trip, a new business idea, or the opportunity to spend more time with family—without worrying about running out of money.

Retirement isn't a one-size-fits-all experience. Some will want to maintain a modest lifestyle with minimal financial stress. Others will want to push the boundaries of what's possible. But what everyone has in common is the need for a plan—one that ensures they can live life on their own terms. The best retirement strategy isn't just about numbers on a spreadsheet. It's about creating a life where money is no longer the limiting factor.

The best time to start planning for retirement was 20 years ago. The second-best time is today. Whether you're just beginning your career, mid-way through, or nearing retirement, there are actions you can take right now to improve your financial future. If you're young, the priority is investing—time is your biggest advantage. If you're mid-career, optimizing retirement accounts and reducing unnecessary expenses can make a huge difference. If you're close to retirement, focusing on cash flow, risk management, and withdrawal strategies is key.

Retirement isn't about stopping work. It's about having the freedom to choose what's next. The decisions you make today will determine whether your future is one of stress and scarcity or one of abundance and choice. The goal isn't just to retire—it's to retire **well**.

You've spent years saving for retirement—but how do you protect that wealth once you have it? One unexpected event—an illness, a lawsuit, or even a home disaster—can wipe out decades of savings. This is why insurance isn't just a 'nice-to-have'—it's a crucial tool for preserving your financial security.

THE IMPORTANCE OF INSURANCE IN

Chapter 10 - How to Protect Yourself Without Overpaying

Nick had always been the kind of person who believed he was in control. A high-earning tech executive with a seven-figure portfolio, he was convinced he didn't need insurance. It wasn't arrogance—just math. He had run the numbers, read the articles, listened to financial pundits who scoffed at over-insuring. "I'm self-insured," he would say, a phrase that had an air of invincibility. Insurance, in his mind, was for people who couldn't afford to take a hit. If his car got wrecked, he could replace it. If his house burned down, he had enough in liquid assets to rebuild. If he got sick, well, that was unlikely—he was in great shape, ate well, and went to the gym five times a week.

And then one morning, he woke up unable to move his left leg.

It started as a tingling sensation the night before, something he dismissed as overdoing it at the squat rack. By sunrise, it was clear something was very wrong. Within hours, he was in an emergency room undergoing tests. A spinal lesion, the doctors said. Could be temporary, could be permanent. More tests were needed. Nick's concern was not just his body, but the sudden realization that every medical scan, every night in the hospital, every specialist visit came with a price tag.

Within a week, Nick was looking at a $140,000 bill. His employer-provided health insurance—something he barely paid attention to before—had a high deductible, co-pays, and out-of-network fees that meant he was responsible for tens of thousands of dollars upfront. His plan covered hospital stays, but not the high-cost specialists he had opted to see. His savings could cover it, of course. That wasn't the issue. The issue was the sudden drain of cash on an event he hadn't planned for.

This is the fallacy of being "self-insured." It sounds reasonable—until life introduces a variable you didn't account for. Nick's story isn't unique. Plenty of high-net-worth individuals believe they don't need insurance because they have enough wealth to absorb a crisis. But wealth doesn't eliminate risk; it simply changes the way risk manifests. Insurance isn't just an expense—it's a risk-transfer strategy. It doesn't just prevent financial ruin; it prevents liquidity crises, forced asset sales, and the emotional stress of navigating a catastrophe without a safety net.

People often think about wealth in terms of what they accumulate. But smart financial planning is just as much about protecting what you've built as it is about growing it. That's where insurance comes in.

What Insurance Really Is (And What It's Not)

There's a fundamental misunderstanding about insurance, and it starts with how people frame it. Most see it as a financial drain—something they pay for but never use, like a gym membership that sits untouched after January. This perception makes insurance feel like a scam, a system designed to enrich companies at the expense of individuals. The reality, however, is that insurance isn't about immediate returns; it's about protecting against catastrophic losses that could erase years of financial progress.

Imagine two people: One views insurance as an expense to minimize, always opting for the lowest coverage possible. The other sees it as an essential component of financial stability. They both go through life without needing it—until one day, one of them does. The first person is forced to sell their home, deplete their retirement savings, and go into debt. The second person? They pay their deductible and move on. The difference between these two outcomes isn't luck—it's preparation.

Think of insurance like a seatbelt. You don't buckle up because you expect to crash every time you drive. You do it because if the unexpected happens, you want to survive with as little damage as possible. Insurance works the same way. You're not buying coverage because you're planning for disaster—you're buying it because if disaster strikes, you want to control how much it costs you.

And this isn't just about the extreme cases. Insurance isn't just about preventing financial ruin—it's about avoiding unnecessary financial setbacks. The money you lose in an uninsured event isn't just the loss; it's also the opportunity cost of what that money could have done for you if it hadn't been drained by a single event.

This brings us to the biggest unpredictable expense of them all: your health.

Health Insurance – Your Biggest Unpredictable Expense

If there's one financial risk most people underestimate, it's medical costs. The #1 cause of personal bankruptcy in North America isn't reckless spending or bad investments—it's medical debt. And this problem doesn't just affect people with low incomes or no savings. Even wealthy individuals have been financially devastated by unexpected health crises.

It's easy to assume that in Canada, healthcare is "free," and in the U.S., employer-provided plans cover everything. Neither of these assumptions is fully true. In Canada, provincial healthcare only covers basic services. That means prescriptions, dental care, vision, private hospital rooms, and specialized treatments are often out-of-pocket expenses unless you have supplemental insurance. In the U.S., the healthcare system is even more complicated, with costs varying wildly depending on whether care is in-network or out-of-network.

A common refrain among young, healthy people is: "I don't need health insurance. I never get sick." But that's the wrong way to think about it. The real question isn't whether you'll get sick—it's whether you can afford the consequences if you do.

Consider Matt, a 32-year-old personal trainer who prided himself on his fitness. No family history of disease, no chronic conditions. One morning, while biking to work, he was hit by a car. He survived, but he needed surgery, physical therapy, and six months of follow-ups. In total, his medical bills reached $180,000. His health insurance had gaps—he had chosen the lowest-premium plan, not realizing that it came with a $10,000 deductible and co-pays that left him covering a significant portion of the costs himself.

The problem wasn't just the medical expenses. It was the financial ripple effect. Matt couldn't work during his recovery, which meant lost income on top of rising medical bills. Within months, he had drained his emergency fund, maxed out his credit cards, and was forced to take out a loan to keep up with expenses. All because he had underestimated the true financial cost of a health crisis.

Health insurance isn't just about avoiding high medical bills—it's about protecting your earning power. When you're uninsured or underinsured, an injury doesn't just cost you money—it costs you time, opportunity, and financial freedom.

This is why choosing a health insurance plan shouldn't be about picking the cheapest option. It should be about balancing affordability with adequate protection. Here's what matters when selecting a plan:

- **Deductibles**: The amount you have to pay before insurance kicks in. Low premiums often come with high deductibles.
- **Co-pays**: Fixed costs per visit—these add up fast if you need ongoing care.
- **In-network vs. out-of-network care**: Going out-of-network can multiply costs exponentially.

It's easy to ignore these details when you're young and healthy. But the reality is, health crises don't send warnings. The best time to prepare for a medical emergency is before you have one.

You wouldn't drive without car insurance, even if you were a perfect driver. So why gamble on your health?

Life Insurance – The Only Insurance That's Not for You

Most insurance is about protecting *you*—your health, your home, your car, your financial stability. But life insurance is different. It's the only insurance you will never personally use. You will never file a claim, never cash a payout, never see a cent of its benefits. That's because life insurance isn't for you—it's for the people you leave behind.

That distinction makes life insurance one of the most misunderstood financial tools. Many people dismiss it as unnecessary, assuming they won't need it because, well, they'll be dead. But that's precisely the point. The moment you die, life insurance converts into something extraordinary: a tax-free financial lifeline for your loved ones, a final paycheck, a last act of financial responsibility.

To understand life insurance's real purpose, think about it this way: Imagine you could write a check for $1 million to your spouse or children, but the catch is they can only cash it after you're gone. Would you do it? That's exactly what life insurance does—it ensures that your family is not left scrambling financially when you're no longer there to provide for them.

At its core, life insurance serves two main purposes:

1. **Income Replacement for Dependents** – If your family relies on your income, life insurance makes sure they don't suddenly face a financial free fall in your absence. Mortgage payments, education costs, daily living expenses—these don't disappear when you do.
2. **Wealth Transfer Without Taxation** – Life insurance is one of the few assets that can be passed on to beneficiaries tax-free. While investment accounts and real estate often come with tax burdens, a life insurance payout provides immediate liquidity without deductions.

The problem is that most people vastly underestimate how much coverage they actually need. A common assumption is that employer-provided life insurance is enough. Many companies offer a policy that covers one or two years' worth of salary—but that's far from sufficient. If you earn $80,000 a year and your employer gives you a policy worth $160,000, that may seem like a lot. But what happens after two years? If you have a spouse, children, or even aging parents depending on you, that money will be gone faster than you think.

This is where people make another critical mistake: thinking life insurance is only for married people with children. In reality, single people with significant debts or financial obligations should consider coverage, too. If you have a mortgage, co-signed loans, or family members who rely on your financial support, life insurance ensures that these obligations don't become someone else's burden after you're gone.

So, how do you choose the right type of life insurance? It comes down to understanding the three main categories:

- **Term Life Insurance** – This is the simplest and most affordable option. You pay for coverage over a set period—typically 10, 20, or 30 years. If you die during that term, your beneficiaries receive the payout. If you outlive the policy, it expires, and you get nothing. Think of it as "renting" insurance. It's cheap, straightforward, and ideal for most young families.
- **Whole Life Insurance** – Unlike term insurance, whole life policies last your entire lifetime and accumulate a cash value over time. They are significantly more expensive but act as both insurance and an investment vehicle. Some people use them for estate planning or forced savings, but they require careful consideration.
- **Universal Life Insurance** – A more flexible form of permanent insurance, universal life lets you adjust premiums and death benefits. However, it's also more complex and can be risky if not properly managed.

One final counterintuitive thought: If you think you don't need life insurance, ask yourself—who will pay your debts, funeral costs, and remaining financial obligations if you die tomorrow? The answer to that question should determine whether you need coverage.

Homeowners' Insurance - More Than Just a Mortgage Requirement

Most people don't read their home insurance policy until it's too late. It's an afterthought, a box checked off when signing mortgage papers. The assumption is simple: "If something happens to my house, I'm covered." But insurance is never that simple.

Take the case of Rachel, a homeowner in Toronto who had a standard home insurance policy. One night, a major storm caused severe flooding in her neighborhood, damaging the foundation of her home. When she filed a claim, she got a brutal surprise: her policy didn't cover flooding.

Her insurer explained that while fire, wind damage, and even some forms of water damage were covered, flooding required a separate policy. She was on the hook for nearly $80,000 in repairs. Like most homeowners, she had assumed "home insurance" meant protection against everything—but in reality, policies are filled with exclusions that people only discover when they file a claim.

Here's what home insurance actually does:

- **Covers repairs and rebuilding costs after disasters like fire, windstorms, and theft.**
- **Provides liability protection if someone is injured on your property.**
- **Covers temporary living expenses if your home becomes uninhabitable.**

But here's what many people don't realize:

- **Flooding and earthquakes are almost never covered in standard policies.** You need separate policies for those risks.
- **Inflation and supply chain issues have made rebuilding costs skyrocket.** Many homeowners are underinsured without realizing it. A policy that was enough to rebuild a home five years ago may now leave you short.
- **Renters need insurance, too.** Many assume that if they don't own a home, they don't need insurance. But renters' insurance protects **your belongings** (furniture, electronics, clothing) and offers liability coverage in case of accidents.

A counterintuitive insight: You don't buy home insurance for the house—you buy it to protect everything you've built inside it. The walls and roof are replaceable; the financial foundation of your life is not.

Auto Insurance - Understanding What You're Actually Paying For

Why do some people with spotless driving records see their auto insurance premiums go up every year? It seems unfair. You've never had an accident, never made a claim—so why are you paying more?

Here's the secret: Your insurance rate isn't just about you—it's about everyone around you.

Insurance companies don't price policies based on individual drivers alone. They use risk pools, which means your rate is partly determined by the claims history of everyone else in your area. If accidents and claims increase in your city—even if you weren't involved—your premium can go up because insurers adjust pricing based on rising risks.

Auto insurance is made up of several components:

- **Liability Insurance** – Covers damage and injuries you cause to other people.
- **Collision Coverage** – Pays for repairs to your car after an accident.
- **Comprehensive Coverage** – Covers non-accident-related damage like theft, vandalism, or weather-related incidents.

Most drivers assume they're fully covered because they meet the legal minimums. But the reality is minimum liability coverage is rarely enough. If you cause a serious accident, the costs can easily exceed legal minimums, leaving you personally responsible for the remaining damages.

For example, if your province or state requires only $50,000 in liability coverage, but you cause a crash that results in $500,000 in medical bills and lawsuits, guess who's paying the remaining $450,000? You are.

A common mistake: People think auto insurance is about protecting their car. It's not. Your car is replaceable—your financial future is not. The real purpose of auto insurance is to ensure that a single accident doesn't wipe out your savings, force you into debt, or derail your long-term financial goals.

So the next time you see your premium go up, don't just complain—ask yourself: What would happen if I had to cover a major accident out of pocket? That's the real cost of going without the right coverage.

The One Policy That Covers Everything Else – Umbrella Insurance

If there's one financial disaster most people never see coming, it's a lawsuit. It doesn't matter if you're an everyday professional, a small business owner, or a high-income earner—when a lawyer sees dollar signs, your financial stability is suddenly on trial.

Consider the case of Adam, a 42-year-old consultant from Vancouver. One winter evening, he was driving home from a late meeting when he hit a pedestrian at a crosswalk. It was dark, the roads were slick, and the pedestrian had stepped out just as the light changed. The injuries were severe. Adam's auto insurance covered $500,000 in liability, but the victim's medical expenses, lost wages, and pain and suffering claim added up to $2.3 million. When the judgment came down, Adam was on the hook for the remaining $1.8 million. His savings were wiped out. He had to sell his house. His wages were garnished.

Now, here's the thing: Adam wasn't reckless. He wasn't underinsured in the way most people think. He had what he assumed was "good" auto insurance. But he didn't have umbrella insurance—a policy specifically designed to cover the catastrophic financial shortfall that occurs when a lawsuit exceeds normal policy limits.

Most people assume umbrella insurance is something reserved for the ultra-rich, for people with sprawling estates and luxury cars. But the truth is, anyone with a home, savings, or a decent salary is at risk. If you have assets, you have something a lawyer can come after. And in a world where lawsuits can stretch into the millions, standard home and auto policies often aren't enough.

Here's how umbrella insurance works:

- It kicks in after you exhaust the limits of your existing home or auto policy.
- It covers massive legal judgments that would otherwise destroy your finances.
- It protects against lawsuits for accidents, property damage, and even personal liability cases like defamation or false arrest.

The most counterintuitive part of umbrella insurance? It's shockingly cheap. For about $150–$300 per year, a $1 million umbrella policy can mean the difference between financial ruin and walking away unscathed. That's less than what most people pay for a streaming service, yet it's the one policy that protects against the kind of lawsuits that could obliterate decades of savings.

And here's the kicker: The more successful you become, the more at risk you are. Wealth doesn't just bring security—it also makes you a target. If you earn a high salary, own property, or have significant assets, a lawsuit against you will likely be for everything you have, not just what your insurance covers.

Think of umbrella insurance like the roll cage inside a race car. You hope you'll never need it. You hope your existing insurance will be enough. But if you ever get into a catastrophic wreck—financially speaking—it's the only thing that keeps everything from collapsing on top of you.

The Biggest Insurance Mistakes People Make

For something as critical as financial protection, most people make shocking mistakes when it comes to insurance. Some are innocent oversights. Others are the result of bad advice, flawed assumptions, or the temptation to save a few dollars today at the cost of catastrophic loss tomorrow.

Mistake #1 - Choosing the Cheapest Policy Instead of the Right One

Nobody wants to overpay for insurance, but going for the lowest premium without considering coverage is like buying a parachute based on price instead of quality. Sure, you saved money—until the moment you actually need it.

Consider home insurance. Many policies advertise low premiums but quietly cap payout limits below what it actually costs to rebuild a house. If your home burns down, and you're left with a check for $300,000 when the real rebuilding cost is $500,000, guess who covers the shortfall? You do.

Mistake #2 - Not Understanding Exclusions and Coverage Limits

Most people assume their insurance covers them for all major risks. But policies are filled with exclusions. Standard home insurance doesn't cover flooding. Auto insurance won't pay for personal belongings stolen from your car. Health insurance might not cover an experimental treatment, even if it's the only option.

Reading the fine print isn't exciting, but it's the difference between thinking you're insured and actually being insured.

Mistake #3 - Failing to Update Policies as Life Circumstances Change

Insurance isn't a one-time decision. Life changes—marriage, kids, a new home, a growing career—mean your coverage should evolve with you. But many people set their policies and forget about them.

The problem? What was adequate coverage five years ago may be dangerously insufficient today. The result? A policy that *feels* like it's protecting you but, in reality, leaves huge financial gaps.

Mistake #4 -Thinking Employer-Provided Insurance Is Enough

Many employees assume their workplace benefits fully cover them. The reality? Employer-provided life insurance rarely covers more than one or two years of salary, and if you leave your job, you often lose your coverage entirely. It's a benefit, not a full solution.

Mistake #5 - Skipping Umbrella Insurance Because It "Seems Unnecessary"

Most people don't think they'll ever be sued. Most people don't think they'll be responsible for a catastrophic accident. But lawsuits aren't reserved for high-profile celebrities or corporations—they happen to everyday people who were simply in the wrong place at the wrong time.

And the worst time to find out you're underinsured? The moment you need to file a claim.

Most people think of insurance as a necessary evil—something they grudgingly pay for but hope to never use. But that thinking is backward. Insurance isn't about throwing money away. It's about buying back your financial freedom. Consider what financial independence really means. It's not just having wealth. It's having the ability to withstand financial shocks without losing everything you've built. A well-structured insurance plan doesn't just protect your money—it protects your choices, your stability, and your future.

If an unexpected event happened tomorrow—a medical crisis, a lawsuit, a natural disaster—would your finances survive it? Would you be able to continue your life as planned, or would everything unravel overnight? That's the real value of insurance. It's not just about avoiding loss—it's about ensuring that when life throws its worst at you, your financial future remains intact.

Because when you strip everything else away, true financial security isn't about how much money you make. It's about how much you get to keep.

Tax
Deductiont Salary
Retirement savings
Creductiuny
Fevductivns
1455
$ 9,7000
$1 35500
£59
MASTERING TAX EFFICIENCY

Chapter 11 - The Most Overlooked Strategy for Keeping More of Your Money

Dr. James Halvorsen never thought much about taxes. A highly successful dentist, he was far too busy running his practice, managing staff, and squeezing in tee times at the golf course. He made $450,000 a year, more than enough to afford his lakeside home, private school tuition for his kids, and family vacations to Europe. By all measures, he was doing well—until April rolled around.

The first year, he was shocked when his accountant told him he owed nearly $200,000 in taxes. It felt like a gut punch. But instead of adjusting his financial strategy, he did what most people do—he grumbled about how unfair the system was, paid the bill, and moved on. The next year, it happened again. And the year after that.

By the time he hit his mid-40s, James started to notice something troubling. Despite earning nearly half a million dollars a year, he wasn't much wealthier than he had been a decade earlier. His savings weren't growing the way he expected. Investments weren't compounding fast enough. And worse, whenever he looked at the net earnings his colleagues in other professions were bringing home—some earning less but keeping more—he realized he had made a mistake. He had ignored the one financial rule every wealthy person follows: It's not about what you make; it's about what you keep.

At a dinner party, he vented his frustration to a friend—another dentist, but one with a very different approach. "I don't understand," James said, refilling his wine glass. "We make the same money. But you seem to have more of it. How?"

His friend leaned back and smiled. "Because I don't just earn. I plan."

Over the next hour, James learned that his friend had structured his earnings strategically—splitting income between personal and corporate structures, maximizing deductions, and leveraging tax-sheltered investments. The result? He legally paid 30% less in taxes than James did. It wasn't that he worked harder or even earned more. He just understood the rules of the tax game and played it better.

That night, James had an epiphany. He wasn't overpaying taxes because the system was unfair. He was overpaying because he had never bothered to learn the system in the first place.

How the Tax System Actually Works (And Why Most People Misuse It)

Most people treat taxes like the weather—an unavoidable force of nature that they have no control over. They assume that taxes are something that just happens to them. In reality, taxes are a structured system of incentives and penalties, designed not just to raise revenue but to guide financial behavior. The people who understand this don't just pay less—they use the system to build wealth.

The biggest misconception? "The more you make, the more taxes you pay." It's technically true, but not in the way most people assume.

Canada and the U.S. both have progressive tax systems, meaning that the more you earn, the higher percentage of your income is taxed. But here's the part most people get wrong: You don't pay your highest tax rate on your entire income.

For example, in the U.S., a single filer earning $100,000 doesn't pay 24% on all of it. Instead, their income is divided into brackets:

- The first $11,000 is taxed at 10%.
- The next $33,725 is taxed at 12%.
- The next $50,650 is taxed at 22%.
- Only the last $4,625 is taxed at 24%.

In Canada, the principle is the same—your earnings move through tax brackets rather than being taxed at a single percentage. The higher the bracket, the more tax-efficient strategies become essential to avoid losing too much to taxation.

Marginal tax rate is the rate you pay on your last dollar earned. If you're in the 24% bracket, that doesn't mean you pay 24% on all your income—just the last portion. Effective tax rate, on the other hand, is the total percentage of your income that actually goes to taxes. It's usually much lower than the highest marginal rate.

For example, if someone earns $100,000 and pays $18,000 in total tax, their effective tax rate is 18%, not 24%.

This misunderstanding leads many people to make bad financial decisions, like avoiding earning more for fear of "moving into a higher bracket," when in reality, the extra income is still mostly theirs to keep.

When people hear about tax savings, their minds often leap to shadowy offshore accounts, billionaire loopholes, or aggressive write-offs that invite an audit. But the truth is far less dramatic. The best tax-saving strategies aren't loopholes at all—they're government incentives designed to encourage behavior that benefits the economy. Governments don't want you to cheat the system; they want you to use the system to its fullest potential.

The people who pay the least in taxes aren't criminals—they're planners. They understand that tax codes are filled with legal ways to keep more of what you earn, and most of them are incredibly simple to use. Yet the vast majority of taxpayers never take advantage of all the breaks available to them—not because they can't, but because they don't even know they exist.

Tax Deductions vs. Tax Credits – What's the Difference?

Most people lump all tax breaks into one category, but there's a big difference between deductions and credits. Understanding this distinction is one of the fastest ways to lower your tax bill.

Deductions reduce taxable income—the amount the government calculates your tax from. The lower your taxable income, the less you owe. Think of deductions like discounts on a high-end purchase. If you can knock $20,000 off your taxable income, you might save $5,000 in taxes, depending on your tax rate.

Credits reduce actual tax owed—a dollar-for-dollar reduction in your bill. If you get a $2,000 tax credit, that's $2,000 less you owe, no calculations needed. Think of credits like cash rebates: a direct benefit that puts money back in your pocket.

Here's the easiest way to remember it: Deductions lower the price of admission. Credits refund part of the ticket.

Most taxpayers leave money on the table simply because they don't know what they qualify for. Here's a quick look at some of the biggest tax breaks in Canada and the U.S. that go **underutilized.**

United States

- **Mortgage Interest Deduction** - Homeowners can deduct interest paid on their mortgage (up to a limit).
- **SALT Deductions** - State and local taxes paid (property, income, or sales tax) can be deducted—capped at $10,000.
- **Student Loan Interest** - Up to $2,500 of interest paid on student loans can be deducted.
- **Medical Expenses** - Any unreimbursed medical expenses above **7.5% of adjusted gross income** can be deducted.
- **Charitable Contributions** - Donations to qualifying nonprofits can be deducted—sometimes up to 60% of income.

Canada

- **RRSP Contributions** - Contributions to a Registered Retirement Savings Plan reduce taxable income—one of the biggest tax advantages available.
- **Home Office Deduction** - Self-employed workers and remote employees can deduct expenses related to working from home.
- **Tuition & Student Loan Interest** - Canadians can claim credits for tuition and deduct student loan interest.
- **Childcare Expenses** - Daycare, babysitting, and other childcare costs are tax-deductible up to certain limits.
- **GST/HST Rebates** - Low-to-moderate income Canadians qualify for a tax-free quarterly payment.

Most people don't claim all the tax breaks they qualify for because they don't realize they exist. Many assume their accountant is handling everything. But tax professionals focus on compliance first, optimization second. Knowing what to ask for is half the battle.

Tax-Efficient Investing – How to Keep More of What You Earn

The difference between a good investor and a great investor isn't just how much their portfolio grows—it's how much of that growth they actually keep.

Two people can earn the same investment returns, but the one who pays less tax on their profits will always win in the long run.

Most people earn their money through salaries or wages. But wealthy individuals rely on investment income—not just because it grows, but because it's taxed differently.

- Ordinary Income (wages, salaries) is taxed at the highest rates.
- Capital Gains (profits from selling investments) are taxed at lower rates, especially if held long-term (over a year).

This is why Warren Buffett famously pays a lower tax rate than his secretary. His wealth doesn't come from a paycheck—it comes from investments taxed at lower rates.

In Canada, investors love the Dividend Tax Credit, which makes dividend income more tax-efficient than regular salary income. In the U.S., municipal bonds are popular because their interest income is tax-free at the federal level. Your tax rate isn't just about how much you make—it's about how you make it.

Investors tend to focus on gains, but smart investors know how to use losses to their advantage.

Tax-loss harvesting is the practice of selling investments at a loss to offset taxable gains elsewhere. If you have a $5,000 gain from selling a stock, but also sell another stock for a $5,000 loss, your taxable gain drops to zero—eliminating taxes owed. In the U.S., losses can offset up to $3,000 of other income per year, with the rest carried forward. In Canada, capital losses can be carried back three years or forward indefinitely to offset future gains.

This is why December is the busiest tax-planning month for investors—people sell underperforming stocks to lower their tax bills before year-end.

Most investors obsess over picking the right stocks, but asset location—where you hold investments—can be even more important.

- **Taxable Accounts** - Stocks with long-term capital gains and tax-efficient ETFs.
- **Tax-Free Accounts (TFSA, Roth IRA)** - Growth stocks and high-return investments.
- **Tax-Deferred Accounts (RRSP, 401(k))** - Bonds, REITs, or anything producing taxable interest.

Holding the right investments in the wrong accounts can mean paying thousands more in taxes.

How the Wealthy Pay Less Tax (And What You Can Learn from Them)

There is a common myth that the rich avoid taxes through a labyrinth of offshore accounts, shadowy loopholes, or outright tax evasion. The reality is far less scandalous and far more practical. Wealthy people don't evade taxes—they structure their income in ways that reduce their tax burden legally. The best part? These strategies aren't just for billionaires. Many of them can be applied by anyone who understands the tax code well enough to use it to their advantage.

Most people earn money through salaries and wages, which are taxed at the highest possible rates. The wealthy, on the other hand, avoid this trap by focusing on income that is taxed more favorably, such as business profits, investments, and real estate. They don't just work for money—they make money work for them in the most tax-efficient way possible.

To understand how the wealthy pay less tax, consider two individuals: John, a high-earning employee, and Sarah, a high-earning investor.

John earns a six-figure salary of $250,000 a year. His income is subject to the highest tax rates because it's earned income—meaning he pays federal tax, state/provincial tax, payroll tax, and other deductions before he even sees his paycheck. His tax bill might be 40% or more.

Sarah, on the other hand, earns $250,000 a year—but instead of a paycheck, she gets her income through investments, capital gains, and rental properties. Her money is taxed at lower rates because of the following key differences:

- Capital gains tax is lower than income tax. If Sarah holds an investment for over a year before selling, she might only pay 15-20% in tax in the U.S. or 50% of her gains taxed in Canada.
- Dividends from stocks are taxed at reduced rates. Canadian investors enjoy the Dividend Tax Credit, which makes dividend income more attractive than salary.
- Rental property depreciation offsets taxable income. Sarah can deduct property depreciation, reducing her tax bill without actually losing money.

The wealthy don't just work for their money—they structure it in a way that reduces the percentage they give to the government. This is why so many entrepreneurs, real estate investors, and stock market participants end up wealthier than even high-salaried professionals.

For business owners and freelancers, incorporation is one of the most overlooked yet powerful tax strategies. Many professionals—consultants, independent contractors, even doctors and lawyers—continue to pay personal income tax rates on their earnings, even when they could incorporate and pay a much lower corporate tax rate.

Consider this: In the U.S., the top personal tax bracket is 37%, while the corporate tax rate is 21%. In Canada, some small businesses can qualify for a low 9-12% corporate tax rate on the first $500,000 of income. That's an enormous difference.

Why is this important? Because business owners get to choose when they take their income. Instead of earning a salary and getting taxed immediately, an incorporated professional can:

- Leave earnings inside the company, deferring taxes to a later year.

- Pay themselves dividends instead of salary, which is taxed at a lower rate.
- Write off expenses that employees cannot—such as home office costs, travel, and meals.

The result? More control over when and how much tax they pay. This is why wealthy individuals don't just earn money—they control how and when it's taxed.

Most people assume that wealthy individuals donate to charities out of generosity. While that may be partially true, there's another, more practical reason: it's one of the smartest ways to reduce taxes.

Governments encourage charitable giving by offering significant tax incentives—meaning the more you give, the less you owe in taxes. But high earners don't just write a check to charity—they use a Donor-Advised Fund (DAF), a strategy that allows them to:

- Donate a large amount in one year (to get a big tax deduction).
- Keep the money invested and growing tax-free inside the DAF.
- Distribute funds to charities over time, while still controlling the investments.

In other words, they lower their tax bill now while keeping control over their charitable giving for the future.

Counterintuitive insight: The rich don't give to charity because they're generous—they do it because it's the smartest way to lower taxes.

The One-Year Tax Plan – How to Stay Ahead of the Game

Most people treat taxes as an annual event—something they think about for a few weeks before the filing deadline. But the truth is, tax planning is a year-round strategy. The wealthiest individuals and smartest investors don't just file taxes—they plan their financial moves months in advance to minimize tax liability before it happens.

One of the biggest mistakes taxpayers make is waiting until tax season to review their income, deductions, and contributions. By that point, it's too late to make meaningful changes.

Instead of scrambling every April, the most effective tax planners:

- Review their pay stubs, investment income, and deductions every three months.
- Adjust contributions to tax-advantaged accounts before year-end.
- Make strategic purchases (such as business equipment or deductible expenses) before December 31st.

By treating tax planning as a continuous process, they ensure they never overpay due to lack of preparation.

The easiest way to reduce taxes isn't to scramble for receipts at the last minute—it's to automate smart tax moves throughout the year. Set up automatic contributions to tax-advantaged accounts (RRSPs, 401(k)s, TFSAs, IRAs). Use software to track deductible expenses and categorize them as they happen. Schedule end-of-year financial reviews to maximize tax deductions.

Just as great investors automate their savings, great tax planners automate their deductions and contributions.

The fear of getting audited stops many people from being aggressive but legal with their tax planning. The key is knowing what triggers audits:

- Self-employed people with unusually high deductions.
- Large charitable donations that don't match income.
- Inconsistent income reporting (huge changes in earnings year-over-year).

Keep meticulous records of deductions and expenses. Don't exaggerate business write-offs beyond what's reasonable. Match reported income to bank deposits and investment statements. Most audits aren't random—they happen when something doesn't add up. The best defense is accurate documentation.

The tax system isn't designed to punish you—it's designed to incentivize the behaviors the government wants.

- Investing? Lower taxes.
- Starting a business? Lower taxes.
- Donating to charity? Lower taxes.
- Contributing to retirement accounts? Lower taxes.

The difference between overpaying in taxes and keeping more of your wealth isn't about cheating the system. It's about playing the game better.

So, the question is simple: Are you going to be the person who overpays because you didn't plan? Or are you going to be the person who keeps more money by using the same rules the wealthy use?

What's one tax move you can make today that will save you money next year?

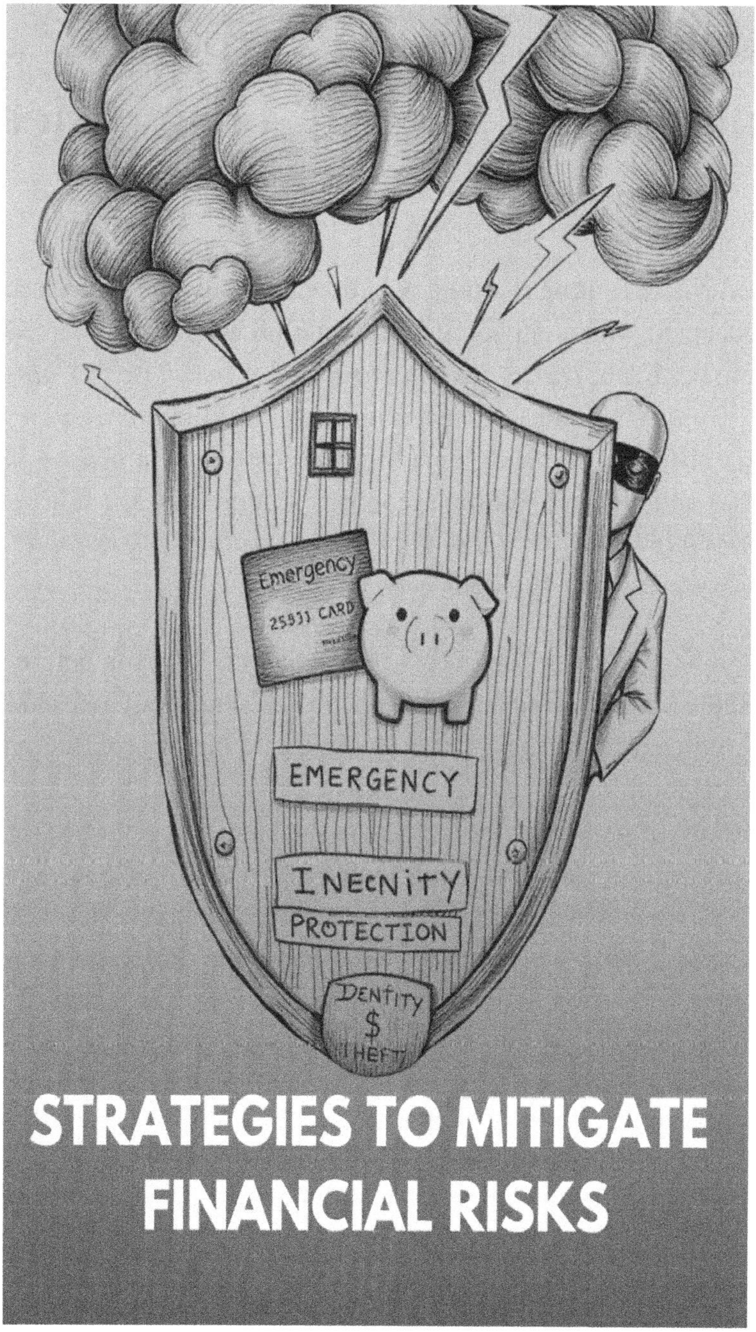
Emergency
25531 CARD
EMERGENCY
INECNITY
PROTECTION
DENTITY
$
STRATEGIES TO MITIGATE FINANCIAL RISKS

Chapter 12 - How to Prepare for the Unexpected Without Losing Sleep

It started with a routine morning. Claire was running late for work, her mind occupied with an upcoming presentation, when she received a text from her bank: *Did you authorize a $4,800 purchase in California? Reply YES or NO.* Claire frowned. She lived in Edmonton, had never been to California, and hadn't made any recent large purchases. She typed **NO** and hit send. Within seconds, a second message followed: *Your card has been frozen due to suspicious activity. Please call customer service to verify your account.*

It took an hour of frustrating back-and-forth with the bank before she realized the severity of what had happened. A fraudster had used her stolen credit card information to make multiple purchases. But that was just the beginning. By the time she checked her email, she found notifications of password reset requests she hadn't made. Then, her phone service stopped working. The fraudster had called her mobile provider, impersonated her, and transferred her number to a new SIM card—locking her out of every account that relied on text message verification.

The next few months were a nightmare. Someone had applied for a car loan in her name, maxed out a line of credit she hadn't even known existed, and left her with thousands of dollars in fraudulent debt. The worst part wasn't the money—her bank refunded most of the fraudulent transactions. It was the time. Claire spent six months untangling the mess, fighting to restore her credit score, proving that she hadn't racked up debt she never saw. It was exhausting.

By the time she recovered, she wasn't the same person. She no longer trusted online banking the way she once had. She became paranoid about emails, double-checked every charge on her credit card, and set up alerts for the smallest financial transactions. Claire had learned the hard way that identity theft isn't just about losing money—it's about losing control.

People assume that identity theft is a rare, unfortunate event that happens to reckless people who share too much information online. The truth is that it's shockingly common, indiscriminate, and easier for criminals than ever before.

The shift to digital transactions has turned everyone into a potential target. Just a decade ago, stealing someone's identity required effort—it meant intercepting mail, digging through trash for sensitive documents, or physically stealing a wallet. Today, all it takes is a single weak password, a hacked database, or a phishing email for cybercriminals to gain access to bank accounts, tax returns, or credit applications.

Consider these staggering facts.

- Identity theft is now the fastest-growing financial crime in North America. In the U.S. alone, there were over *1.1 million cases of identity theft reported in 2023—a 60% increase over five years.*
- The average victim takes *six months* to recover from financial fraud. Fixing stolen credit, disputing fraudulent loans, and repairing the damage can become a full-time job.

- Data breaches are no longer rare events. In 2024, over *400 million personal records* were exposed through hacks, leaks, and phishing scams. If you've ever given your email to a bank, online retailer, or subscription service, your information is likely floating somewhere on the dark web.

Here's what makes it even worse: Most people won't realize they've been compromised until months later. The person stealing your identity isn't going to drain your account all at once—that would trigger an immediate alert. Instead, they start small. A few dollars here. A minor change of address request there. By the time they've maxed out your credit, taken out a fraudulent loan, or impersonated you on a tax return, the damage is deep.

Most identity theft cases could have been prevented with a few simple security measures.

How to Reduce Your Risk of Identity Theft

1. **Monitor Your Financial Accounts Like a Hawk**

Most identity theft victims say the same thing: *I wish I had caught it sooner.* The earlier you detect fraudulent activity, the easier it is to stop the damage. This is why regularly checking your bank statements, credit reports, and transaction history is essential.

- **Set up real-time alerts.** Almost every bank and credit card company allows you to receive notifications for transactions over a certain amount.
- **Check your credit report at least twice a year.** In both Canada and the U.S., you're entitled to free credit reports—use them to scan for accounts you don't recognize.

- **Look for "microcharges."** Fraudsters often test stolen cards by charging a small, unnoticeable amount ($1-$5) before making big purchases.

2. **Secure Your Digital Identity with Stronger Passwords and 2FA**

Cybercriminals **love weak passwords.** If your go-to password is *Password123* or your pet's name, you're making their job too easy.

- **Use long, unique passwords for every account.** A password like *Giraffe2!CanadaLawnmower67* is nearly impossible to guess.
- **Enable two-factor authentication (2FA).** This adds an extra layer of security by requiring a second step—like a text message or email code—to log in.
- **Avoid using the same password across multiple sites.** If one account is breached, all your accounts become vulnerable.

3. **Freeze Your Credit When Not in Use**

One of the most effective yet underused security measures is **freezing your credit.** When your credit is frozen, no one—including identity thieves—can open a new loan, credit card, or mortgage in your name.

- **In Canada:** Contact Equifax Canada and TransUnion to request a **credit lock.**
- **In the U.S.:** The three major bureaus—Equifax, Experian, and TransUnion—allow you to freeze and unfreeze your credit for free.

Think of this as **locking the front door to your financial identity.** If someone tries to open a fraudulent credit account in your name, they'll be denied.

4. **Avoid Phishing Scams and Public Wi-Fi Risks**

If you've ever received an email from "your bank" asking you to reset your password immediately, you've been targeted by a **phishing scam.** These scams impersonate trusted companies to trick you into handing over personal information.

- **Red flag:** Banks, government agencies, and legitimate companies **never** ask for sensitive information over email or text.
- **How to check:** Hover over links before clicking—if the URL looks suspicious, **don't click.**
- **Public Wi-Fi:** Never log into financial accounts on public networks (coffee shops, airports, etc.) unless using a **VPN.** Hackers can intercept your connection and steal your login details.

The Identity Theft Recovery Plan (If You Get Hacked)

Despite all precautions, sometimes **the worst still happens.** If you ever fall victim to identity theft, **immediate action is crucial.**

Step 1 - Contact your bank and freeze all affected accounts.
Step 2 - Place fraud alerts on your credit reports.
Step 3 - Report the theft to law enforcement and relevant institutions (FTC in the U.S., RCMP in Canada).
Step 4 - Monitor your financial activity **for at least a year**—fraudsters often wait months before attempting another attack.

Most people assume identity theft is about losing money. In reality, the biggest cost isn't financial—it's psychological. Victims of fraud often experience paranoia, anxiety, and a loss of trust in financial systems. The best defense isn't waiting for something to go wrong—it's proactively taking steps before it ever happens.

In the world of personal finance, earning more is important. But keeping what you've earned safe? That's just as critical.

Legal Safeguards – Protecting Your Assets From the Unexpected

It's a story that plays out more often than you'd think. A father of three, Mark, ran a successful small business in Calgary, owned a paid-off home, and had a respectable investment portfolio. He was careful with his money, always saving, always planning for the future. But there was one thing he never got around to—writing a will.

His logic was simple: he wasn't a billionaire, didn't have a sprawling estate, and figured his family would "just sort things out" if something happened to him. After all, his wife and kids knew what he wanted, right?

Then, the unexpected happened. A car accident. A fatal injury. A life cut short in an instant.

And with no legal plan in place, Mark's financial stability unraveled posthumously. His bank accounts were **frozen**. His home went into **probate court**, meaning his family couldn't immediately access or sell it. His business assets were in **legal limbo**, with no clear successor to manage ongoing operations. Worst of all, since Mark never specified who should take custody of his children, the court had to **appoint a guardian**—a decision that took months of legal proceedings.

What should have been a straightforward transition for his family turned into **two years of legal headaches, stress, and mounting legal fees**. His wife was forced to liquidate assets at unfavorable times, just to keep the family afloat while waiting for the courts to distribute Mark's estate. Had he taken an afternoon to draft a simple will, everything would have been different.

Why Wills & Trusts Matter (Even If You're Not a Millionaire)

People assume estate planning is for the ultra-wealthy—something for tycoons with sprawling mansions and stock portfolios worth millions. But here's the reality: if you own anything of value—whether it's a house, a car, a savings account, or a business—you have an estate. And if you don't decide what happens to it, the government will decide for you.

Dying without a will is called dying intestate, and it puts your entire financial legacy in the hands of the legal system. Here's what that means in practice:

- **Government-Controlled Asset Distribution** – The courts will decide who inherits your wealth, following standard legal formulas—not necessarily what you would have wanted.
- **Frozen Accounts & Probate Delays** – Your loved ones may be unable to access your money for months (or even years) while your estate goes through probate.
- **Unexpected Heirs & Family Conflicts** – If you have estranged relatives, they may have legal claims to your estate, even if you had no intention of leaving them anything.

- **Custody Uncertainty for Children** – If you have minor children and no designated guardian, the court will decide who raises them.

Estate planning isn't just about who gets your money. It's about **avoiding chaos.**

The ultra-wealthy don't just have wills—they have trusts. A trust is a legal entity that holds assets for beneficiaries and distributes them under conditions you set. It's one of the biggest financial secrets of the rich, and it's not just for the elite.

Here's why trusts matter:

- **Avoid Probate** – Assets in a trust don't go through probate, meaning your heirs get access faster.
- **Protect Against Lawsuits** – A trust can protect assets from creditors, ex-spouses, or legal claims.
- **Control Inheritance Timing** – You can decide when and how heirs receive their inheritance (e.g., releasing funds at age 25 instead of all at once).

For example, imagine you want to leave money to your 18-year-old son. If that money is simply written into a will, he inherits everything immediately. If it's in a trust, you can delay access until he's 25, or even stipulate that he only gets funds for specific needs like education or a home purchase.

The wealthy don't just leave money to their heirs—they control how it's used.

The Power of Attorney: Who Makes Decisions If You Can't?

A will controls what happens after you die—but what if you become incapacitated? A power of attorney (POA) allows someone to make financial or medical decisions on your behalf if you're unable to. Without one, your family may have to go through lengthy legal processes just to access your accounts or make medical choices on your behalf.

There are two key types:

- **Financial Power of Attorney** – Manages your money, bills, and legal affairs if you're incapacitated.
- **Healthcare Power of Attorney** – Makes medical decisions if you're unable to communicate.

Without these documents, a court may have to appoint someone to manage your affairs—who may not be the person you would have chosen.

Many people assume estate planning is expensive and complicated. In reality, it can be surprisingly simple and affordable.

- **DIY Wills -** If your estate is straightforward (e.g., you're leaving everything to your spouse and kids), you can use an online will service like **LegalZoom (U.S.) or Willful (Canada)** for around $100.
- **Lawyer-Prepared Wills -** If you have a business, multiple properties, or complex assets, hiring an estate lawyer (typically $500-$2,000) is worth it.

Your estate plan should be updated when major life events happen:

- Marriage or divorce
- Having children

- Buying property
- Receiving an inheritance
- Starting a business

A good rule of thumb: Review your will every five years—even if nothing big has changed.

Why Wealthy People Structure Their Assets Differently

The rich don't just make money differently—they **protect it differently.**

Owning assets in your name makes you personally liable for lawsuits, debts, and taxes. That's why business owners and investors hold assets through legal entities like LLCs or corporations.

- **Tax Advantages** – Corporations and LLCs often pay lower taxes than individuals.
- **Lawsuit Protection** – Personal assets are shielded from business-related lawsuits.
- **Estate Planning Perks** – Ownership can be transferred smoothly to heirs without triggering estate taxes.

This is why the wealthiest individuals own nothing—but control everything.

Most people think financial success is about making smart investments. But history shows that the biggest risk to wealth isn't market crashes—it's a lack of planning.

Families lose fortunes not because they invested poorly, but because they didn't protect what they had. Estate planning isn't about dying—

it's about ensuring that everything you've worked for is safeguarded while you're alive.

The biggest financial disasters aren't stock market crashes. They're the unexpected: sudden illness, accidents, legal battles. The difference between those who build lasting wealth and those who lose it overnight isn't how much they make—it's how well they prepare for what could go wrong.

Final challenge: What's one financial risk you can start protecting yourself against today? If you don't have a will, write one. If you don't have power of attorney, set one up. The greatest mistake isn't making a bad investment—it's failing to protect the ones you've already made.

HARNESSING
REAL ESTATE FOR
FINANCIAL GROWTH
FOR
RENT

Chapter 13 - Why Property Is Still the Middle Class's Best Bet

When Ahmed graduated from pharmacy school in Toronto, he thought he had life figured out. He had done everything by the book—excelled in high school, pushed through years of grueling academics, and secured a job that paid him six figures straight out of university. At 28, he walked into a real estate office, signed the paperwork on a pre-construction condo, and beamed as the agent handed him the keys to his "first investment." It was a one-bedroom unit in a rapidly growing neighborhood, and everyone told him it was a smart move.

For years, Ahmed relished the idea of being a homeowner. His parents were proud, his friends admired his discipline, and his colleagues—many of whom were still renting—saw him as someone who had "made it." But after a decade of paying down his mortgage, covering rising maintenance fees, and battling Toronto's skyrocketing property taxes, he noticed something unsettling: his bank account wasn't growing. In fact, despite his impressive salary, he was treading water financially.

It wasn't that he was irresponsible with money—far from it. He had diligently contributed to his RRSP, avoided frivolous spending, and even dabbled in index funds. But the numbers told an uncomfortable truth: owning his condo hadn't made him wealthy. If anything, it had tied up most of his cash flow in a property that demanded more from him than it gave in return. Meanwhile, a former classmate who had taken a different approach—buying small rental properties instead of a primary residence—was now pulling in an extra $10,000 a month in passive income.

That's when Ahmed had a realization that many people never reach: buying a home is not the same as investing in real estate. It feels like an investment because it's a large purchase that grows in value over time, but in reality, it's an expense—one that locks up your money and leaves you vulnerable to market downturns. Real estate investors don't just "own property"—they generate income from it. They don't see houses as status symbols; they see them as cash-producing assets.

Ahmed had unknowingly bought into a financial illusion, a belief system passed down through generations: *Get a good job. Buy a house. Pay it off. Retire rich.* But if that were truly a wealth-building formula, why were so many homeowners still struggling financially? And why were real estate investors—who owned properties they didn't even live in—growing their wealth exponentially while he remained stuck?

Understanding the Real Estate Wealth Formula

Ask most people what makes real estate valuable, and they'll give you the same answer: location, location, location. It's the golden rule of real estate, repeated so often that it's become gospel. And yet, this mantra—while partly true is also dangerously incomplete.

Yes, location matters. But if location alone created wealth, then every homeowner in a prime area would be financially independent. The reality is that thousands of people own property in expensive cities, yet they still live paycheck to paycheck. The real key to real estate wealth isn't just location—it's strategy.

The average person believes real estate success works like this:

1. Buy a house in a good area.
2. Wait for it to appreciate.
3. Sell it years later for a profit.

This is not an investment strategy. This is speculation disguised as wisdom. It assumes that property values always rise (they don't), that appreciation alone creates wealth (it doesn't), and that simply holding onto real estate guarantees financial success (it won't).

Wealthy real estate investors follow a different formula—one built on four pillars:

1. **Cash Flow** – The monthly rental income that remains after covering all property expenses (mortgage, taxes, maintenance). A property with strong cash flow means you get paid every month, regardless of what the market does.
2. **Appreciation** – While property values tend to rise over the long term, strategic investors don't gamble on appreciation alone. They buy properties that offer immediate value—ones they can improve, refinance, or rent out profitably.
3. **Leverage** – Unlike stocks, real estate allows you to **control a large asset with a small amount of money.** If you invest $50,000 in stocks, that's the total value of your investment. But if you put $50,000 down on a rental property, you can control a $250,000 asset—giving you five times the purchasing power.
4. **Tax Benefits** – Real estate investors enjoy tax advantages that regular homeowners don't. Depreciation, interest deductions, and expense write-offs can significantly reduce taxable income. In some cases, investors even pay **zero tax** on rental profits.

Now, think about how these four pillars interact. If you own a rental property:

- You **receive cash flow** from tenants.
- The property **appreciates over time**, increasing your equity.
- You **use leverage** to acquire more properties without needing millions in cash.
- Your **tax burden is lower** than someone earning the same income from a salaried job.

Walk through any upscale neighborhood, and you'll see rows of million-dollar homes with well-manicured lawns and luxury cars in the driveway. It's easy to assume that the people inside are rich. But wealth isn't about what you own—it's about how much of your money is working for you.

A house that you live in doesn't work for you. It doesn't generate monthly income. It doesn't appreciate in value in a predictable, controllable way. And—perhaps most importantly—it doesn't offer financial flexibility. If you lose your job, you still owe the mortgage. If the market crashes, you can't suddenly turn your house into a liquid asset.

Real estate investors think differently. Their priority isn't owning homes—it's owning income streams. They see property not as a personal achievement, but as a tool to build wealth. That's why they don't just buy houses—they buy rental properties.

Consider two people:

- **Homeowner A** buys a $750,000 condo in Vancouver. He puts down 20%, securing a mortgage for the rest. His monthly costs (mortgage, taxes, maintenance) total $3,500. The condo rises in value over time, but for now, he's paying out of pocket every month with no extra income.

- **Investor B** buys a $750,000 triplex in a mid-sized city. He also puts down 20%, but instead of paying out of pocket, he collects $5,000 in rent from tenants. After expenses, he has $1,500 of positive cash flow per month, plus all the same appreciation benefits as Homeowner A.

Ten years later, Homeowner A might have a property worth $1 million, but he had to cover all the costs himself. Investor B also has a property worth $1 million, but he never paid the mortgage out of pocket—his tenants did. He also collected over $180,000 in rental income over that decade.

Same real estate market. Same initial investment. Radically different outcomes.

The Three Main Paths to Real Estate Wealth

Real estate wealth isn't built in a straight line. There is no universal playbook, no single strategy that works for everyone. Some investors swear by the slow and steady approach of buy-and-hold rentals, others thrive in the high-stakes world of flipping, and then there are those who prefer the completely passive approach of REITs—essentially investing in real estate without ever setting foot in a property. Each path has its own risks, rewards, and requirements. But the biggest mistake? Believing that you have to get it exactly right from the start.

Most first-time investors get paralyzed by indecision. They analyze deals, listen to podcasts, run numbers on mortgage calculators—and then do nothing. They convince themselves that their first purchase needs to be the perfect deal. But real estate isn't about perfection; it's about learning the game. The first property is rarely the one that makes you rich. It's the one that teaches you how to think like an investor.

Option 1 - Buy & Hold Rental Properties (Long-Term Wealth)

Owning a rental property is the classic real estate play. Buy a property, rent it out, and let your tenants pay down the mortgage while you pocket the leftover cash flow. Over time, as rents rise and the loan gets paid off, you build equity—and if you've chosen well, the property appreciates. This is how wealth is built slowly but predictably. It's how millions of people have become financially independent without ever working a high-paying job.

But there's a dangerous myth in real estate: *If you buy a rental property, you'll make money.* The reality? Most rental properties are not profitable. Many first-time landlords run their numbers poorly, failing to account for things like maintenance, vacancies, or rising property taxes. They assume that as long as rent covers the mortgage, they're in good shape. But a truly great rental property does more than just cover costs—it provides positive cash flow. That means after paying all expenses, you still walk away with money every month.

Here's how seasoned investors evaluate a rental deal:

- **Cash Flow:** Does the property generate at least $200–$500 in monthly profit after covering mortgage, taxes, insurance, and maintenance?
- **Rent-to-Price Ratio:** A good rule of thumb is the **1% rule**—if monthly rent is at least 1% of the purchase price, the property is worth considering.

- **Tenant Quality:** A beautiful property in a bad rental market is useless. A great tenant in a less-than-perfect property? That's a winning formula.

Market conditions also matter. Canada's high property prices and strict lending rules make single-family rentals less viable—so investors often turn to multi-family units or secondary suites to maximize cash flow. In contrast, the U.S. offers easier financing, a wider selection of cash-flowing properties, and lower barriers to entry. A Canadian investor might need to spend $1 million to break into the market, whereas an American investor can start with $150,000.

The biggest mistake first-time landlords make? Thinking they need the perfect rental to get started. Buying a rental isn't about getting rich overnight. It's about learning how to run a profitable investment while minimizing risk. The first property teaches you how to screen tenants, negotiate with contractors, and manage cash flow. The second property builds confidence. By the third, you're no longer thinking like a homeowner—you're thinking like an investor.

Option 2 - Fix & Flip (Active Wealth Building)

Flipping houses sounds easy. Buy a run-down property, renovate it, and sell it for a profit. HGTV makes it look like a simple formula: distressed house + renovation = instant wealth. But real estate flipping is not about hammers and paintbrushes—it's about numbers and negotiation. The best flippers aren't home renovators; they're deal-makers who know how to buy low and sell high.

Here's what actually determines a successful flip:

1. **Purchase Price:** The biggest profits are made at the moment of purchase, not at the time of sale. Buying below market value is **non-negotiable.**
2. **Renovation Budget:** Most new flippers underestimate how much repairs cost. A $30,000 budget can easily balloon to $50,000 if you don't control costs.
3. **Selling Price:** A profitable flip requires a strong after-repair value (ARV)—meaning the final selling price must be significantly higher than total costs.

Flipping works best in rising markets where demand is high, and buyers are willing to pay a premium. During a downturn, flippers get stuck holding properties that they can't sell at a profit—or worse, can't sell at all.

Counterintuitively, the most successful flippers are not the ones who fix houses the best—they're the ones who find the best deals. They focus on buying properties below market value, negotiating aggressively, and controlling costs. If you're great at spotting undervalued deals but don't want to handle renovations yourself, you can still make money flipping—by wholesaling properties to other investors for a fee.

Option 3 - REITs & Passive Real Estate Investing

Not everyone wants to be a landlord or take on the risks of flipping. Some investors want the benefits of real estate—without ever dealing with a tenant or a renovation crew. That's where Real Estate Investment Trusts (REITs) come in.

A REIT is essentially a stock that invests in real estate. Instead of owning individual properties, investors buy shares in a company that manages a portfolio of real estate assets—commercial buildings, apartment complexes, industrial warehouses. These REITs generate income through rents, and investors receive dividends—just like collecting rent checks, but without the hassle.

Here's why REITs are an attractive alternative:

- **Liquidity -** Unlike physical real estate, REITs can be bought and sold instantly on the stock market.
- **Diversification -** Instead of owning a single property, you get exposure to an entire portfolio.
- **No Management Required -** No tenants, no repairs, no property taxes—just passive income.

Some of the best-performing REITs focus on high-demand sectors like industrial storage, logistics centers (think Amazon warehouses), and medical facilities. Unlike residential properties, these assets provide stable, long-term cash flow with fewer market fluctuations.

The Smart Investor's Guide to Location & Market Analysis

It's tempting to think that real estate success is all about buying in the right neighborhood. And while location matters, the truth is that timing and market conditions matter just as much. A property in the "best" city can still lose money if bought at the wrong time—or if rental demand isn't strong enough to support its price.

Savvy investors analyze three key factors before making a move:

1. **Job Growth & Population Trends:** Areas with strong job markets attract renters, increasing demand for housing.

2. **Rent-to-Price Ratios:** A $500,000 home that only rents for $1,500/month is a bad deal. The higher the rental yield, the better the cash flow.
3. **Supply vs. Demand:** Some cities have housing shortages (rising prices, strong rental demand), while others have an oversupply of rentals (high vacancies, lower returns).

Markets go through periods of expansion (rising prices), stability (plateauing values), and contraction (declining prices). The best time to buy? During downturns, when assets are undervalued. The worst time? At market peaks, when everyone is scrambling to buy.

Smart investors also use boots-on-the-ground research. Instead of relying solely on online data, they visit potential markets, speak with property managers, and look for signs of rental demand—occupied apartment buildings, new job postings, high walkability scores. Some use the Drive-Test Method—physically visiting neighborhoods, observing properties, and speaking with local landlords.

The best investments aren't always in the biggest cities. Sometimes, suburban and secondary markets offer the highest returns. Investors who look beyond trendy urban centers often find undervalued opportunities hiding in plain sight.

Strategy	Buy & Hold Rentals (Long-Term Wealth)	Fix & Flip (Active Wealth Building)	REITs & Passive Real Estate Investing
Core Concept	Purchase a property, rent it out, and build long-term equity while generating rental income.	Buy undervalued properties, renovate them, and sell for a profit.	Invest in a portfolio of real estate assets through publicly traded Real Estate Investment Trusts (REITs).
Profit Potential	Wealth builds over time through appreciation, mortgage paydown, and positive cash flow.	Potential for high short-term profits, but comes with significant risk and market timing dependency.	Consistent dividend income with stock-like liquidity but limited control over assets.
Investment Time Horizon	Long-term (10+ years)	Short-term (3–12 months per flip)	Flexible (can buy and sell anytime)
Risk Level	Moderate – dependent on market conditions, property management, and tenant stability.	High – depends on buying undervalued properties, managing renovation costs, and selling at a profit.	Low – diversified exposure to real estate with no direct management.

Management Effort	Requires tenant management, property maintenance, and financial oversight.	High involvement in sourcing deals, renovation oversight, and market analysis.	No direct management required—fully passive investment.
Market Conditions Favorability	Best in stable or growing rental markets with high occupancy rates.	Best in rising markets where property values increase. Risky in downturns.	Best when interest rates are low and real estate demand is strong.
Key Metrics for Success	- Positive monthly cash flow ($200–$500+ per property). - Rent-to-price ratio (1% rule: $1,000 rent for a $100,000 home). - Strong tenant demand and low vacancy rates.	- Purchase price well below market value. - Strict renovation budget control. - After-repair value (ARV) significantly exceeding total costs.	- Strong dividend yield (3–7%). - Low expense ratios. - REITs focusing on high-demand sectors (industrial, healthcare, logistics).
Common Mistakes	- Underestimating costs (maintenance, vacancies, property taxes). - Buying properties in weak rental markets.	- Overpaying for properties. - Underestimating renovation costs.	- Assuming all REITs perform equally. - Investing in overleveraged

		- Failing to sell before a market downturn.	REITs with high debt.
Who Should Invest?	Investors seeking **steady, long-term wealth growth** and willing to manage properties or hire a property manager.	Investors looking for **active, high-return opportunities** with experience in real estate, renovation, or deal-making.	Hands-off investors who want **real estate exposure without the headaches of property ownership**.

Financing & Leverage – How to Buy Without Having Millions in Cash

Most people assume that buying real estate requires deep pockets, a perfect credit score, and years of saving. The conventional wisdom is straightforward: if you don't have a large down payment, you're not ready to invest. But if that were true, the richest real estate investors wouldn't be the ones who know the market best—they'd simply be the ones who were born rich. And yet, time and time again, some of the biggest real estate fortunes are built by people who start with nothing but knowledge of how leverage works.

Real estate is one of the few asset classes where banks actually want to help you buy more of it. Try walking into a bank and asking for a loan to buy stocks—they'll laugh you out of the building. But ask for a loan to buy property, and suddenly, they're rolling out mortgage programs, offering competitive rates, and letting you put as little as 5% down in some cases. This is because real estate is a tangible, cash-generating asset that banks consider stable—after all, whether markets rise or fall, people still need places to live.

The secret weapon in real estate investing is leverage. If you have $50,000 and you invest it in stocks, that's all you control—$50,000 worth of assets. But if you use that same $50,000 as a 20% down payment on a $250,000 property, you now control a quarter-million-dollar asset. And if that property appreciates 5% in a year, you don't just earn 5% on your $50,000—you earn 5% on $250,000, meaning your actual return is $12,500 instead of just $2,500. That's the 4X Rule—a 20% down payment lets you control 100% of the property's value.

But leverage isn't just about multiplying returns—it's about accessing the market sooner. Many would-be investors wait until they can buy a house in full, only to find that prices have doubled by the time they have enough. Meanwhile, those who understand financing enter the game early, use other people's money (OPM), and ride the wave of long-term appreciation.

Mortgage Options: Canada vs. U.S.

The financing landscape looks different depending on where you live. In Canada, mortgage regulations tend to be stricter. Buyers must pass a stress test, proving they can afford mortgage payments even if rates rise. However, first-time investors can still access CMHC-insured loans, allowing for lower down payments. There are also government incentives, like RRSP home-buying programs, that let Canadians borrow from their retirement savings to invest in property.

In contrast, U.S. mortgage programs offer more flexibility. Investors can secure 30-year fixed-rate mortgages, which provide long-term stability. FHA loans allow for lower down payments, and investment property loans can be structured with interest-only payments—freeing up cash flow to reinvest.

But what if you don't qualify for traditional financing? That's where alternative financing comes in. Private lenders and hard money loans offer short-term capital for real estate deals, though at higher interest rates. More creative investors form joint ventures, pooling money with partners to buy properties they couldn't afford alone.

Real estate isn't reserved for the rich—it's reserved for those who understand financing. Banks don't care if you started with wealth. They care if you know how to use leverage to turn real estate into a cash-generating machine.

Risk Management – Avoiding the Biggest Mistakes Investors Make

There's a reason why so many people fear real estate investing. They've heard horror stories—landlords struggling with nightmare tenants, market crashes wiping out home values, first-time investors losing money. And while these risks are real, they aren't inevitable. Most real estate losses don't happen because real estate is risky. They happen because investors make mistakes that could have been avoided.

The Three Biggest Real Estate Risks

1. **Vacancies – Underestimating Tenant Demand -** A vacant property is a money pit. The biggest mistake first-time investors make is buying in areas where rental demand is weak. A

property can look great on paper, but if you can't find a tenant, you're stuck covering the mortgage yourself. That's why smart investors prioritize high-demand markets over cheap properties.

2. **Negative Cash Flow – The #1 Mistake New Investors Make** - Many first-time investors fall into the trap of overestimating rental income and underestimating expenses. They assume that as long as the mortgage is covered, they're good—but they forget about maintenance, property taxes, vacancies, and emergency repairs. A property that barely breaks even today could easily become a financial burden tomorrow. Cash flow is king—if a property doesn't generate monthly profit, it's not an investment. It's a liability.

3. **Market Downturns – Real Estate Isn't Guaranteed to Go Up -** Real estate isn't a straight lineup. Markets go through cycles. What goes up can come down, and investors who buy at the peak of a market frenzy can find themselves underwater when values drop. But while markets fluctuate, smart investors never rely solely on appreciation—they focus on buying below market value, ensuring cash flow, and having an exit strategy.

The best real estate investors aren't reckless risk-takers. They're risk managers. They understand that long-term success isn't about making high-risk bets—it's about avoiding stupid mistakes.

- **Always Have an Emergency Fund** – If your roof needs replacing or your tenant stops paying, you don't want to be scrambling for cash. A buffer of 3–6 months of expenses ensures that unexpected costs don't turn into financial disasters.

- **Buy Below Market Value** – Real estate wealth starts at the moment of purchase. The better the deal you get upfront, the lower your risk. Buying at a discount provides built-in protection against market downturns.

- **Have an Exit Strategy** – Before you buy, ask yourself: *What's my Plan B?* If you can't sell at a profit, can you rent it out? If it doesn't rent, can you refinance? Smart investors don't just buy properties—they buy flexibility.

For decades, real estate has been the most reliable wealth-building tool for the middle class. It has created more millionaires than any other investment vehicle. And yet, most people never take advantage of it—not because they don't want to, but because they believe they can't.

They think they need to be rich before they invest.
They think they need to have everything figured out before they buy.
They think real estate is too risky, too complicated, too competitive.

The truth? Real estate is a wealth accelerator because it allows ordinary people to leverage small amounts of money into life-changing returns. It rewards those who take the time to understand it. And unlike stocks or crypto—where price movements are unpredictable—real estate is an asset that you can actively control.

So the real question isn't *should* you invest in real estate. The question is, how will you start?

Are you going to buy your first rental property?
Are you going to invest in a REIT?
Are you going to study your local market and spot opportunities?

Real estate isn't a get-rich-quick scheme. But it is the most proven way to build long-term wealth.

TURNING SIDE
VENTURES INTO
WEALTH-BUILDING
OPPORTUNITIES

Chapter 14 - Entrepreneurship and Side Hustles – The Hidden Engine of Wealth

In 2007, two struggling designers in San Francisco faced a problem: they couldn't afford their rent. The city was expensive, their careers weren't taking off, and neither of them had a steady income. With bills piling up, they came up with what seemed like a desperate and temporary solution—renting out an air mattress in their living room to conference attendees in town for a design event. They set up a simple website, called it "Air Bed & Breakfast," and within days, strangers were paying them to sleep on their floor.

By any conventional business logic, this wasn't a startup—it was a scrappy attempt at survival. The idea was weird, small, and unscalable. Who would ever pay to stay in someone's home when hotels existed? Investors laughed them out of the room. Yet, that tiny experiment evolved into Airbnb, a company now worth over $80 billion.

What makes this story fascinating isn't just the rise of a massive company—it's the counterintuitive lesson that goes against everything people assume about starting a business. Airbnb didn't start with millions in funding or a flawless plan. It started as a side hustle—an experiment born out of necessity, with no expectation that it would lead anywhere.

This isn't just Airbnb's story. Countless entrepreneurs—Shopify's Tobias Lütke, Clearco's Michele Romanow, even Amazon's Jeff

Bezos—started with something small and uncertain before it snowballed into something massive. Yet, when most people think about side hustles or starting a business, they believe they need:

- A **perfect idea**
- A **huge investment**
- A **detailed, polished business plan**
- A **dramatic leap into full-time entrepreneurship**

That's not how real wealth-building works. The reality is much simpler—the most successful businesses start as side projects, experiments, or even mistakes. What matters isn't starting big—it's starting at all.

If financial freedom isn't built through salary alone but through ownership and leverage, why aren't more people pursuing side hustles? The answer isn't a lack of opportunity—it's a series of myths that keep people from starting.

The Biggest Myths About Side Hustles and Entrepreneurship

Myth #1: "You need a lot of money to start"

Ask most people why they haven't started a side business, and they'll tell you they don't have enough money. There's an assumption that launching a business requires huge capital—renting office space, hiring staff, or investing in expensive inventory. This belief is outdated.

Some of the most profitable businesses in the world started with under $500.

Take Graham Stephan, a former real estate agent who built a multi-million-dollar brand on YouTube—starting with nothing but an iPhone and free video editing software. Or consider Michele Romanow, who started her first business in university with just a few hundred dollars, selling caviar from sturgeon fish farms before founding Clearco, a financing platform for entrepreneurs.

The real barrier to entry isn't money—it's knowledge and execution. The modern world has eliminated almost every major startup cost:

- You can **launch an online business for under $100**—using Shopify, Substack, or Etsy.
- You can **start consulting or freelancing for free** on platforms like Upwork and Fiverr.
- You can **resell products without inventory** using drop shipping or Amazon FBA.

Most successful side hustlers don't invest thousands upfront—they start with a small, calculated test. They prove an idea works, then scale.

Myth #2: "You need to quit your job and go all in"

The Hollywood version of entrepreneurship goes like this: A frustrated employee quits their job, takes a huge risk, and builds a billion-dollar company. The problem? This almost never happens in real life.

Statistically, entrepreneurs who keep their full-time jobs while starting a business are actually more likely to succeed than those who quit everything. Why? Because they're not under financial pressure to make desperate decisions.

Take Sara Blakely, the billionaire founder of Spanx. She worked as a fax machine salesperson for years while developing her shapewear brand after hours. Or Henry Ford, who spent years working as an engineer at Edison Illuminating Company while perfecting the design for the Model T.

Starting a side hustle while keeping your main job isn't playing it safe—it's playing it smart. You get to experiment, learn, and build income streams without putting your entire financial stability at risk. The modern economy rewards hybrid entrepreneurs—people who straddle both worlds until their business is too big to ignore.

Myth #3: "If it's not making big money fast, it's not worth it"

There's a reason most people give up on side hustles—they assume that if they're not making thousands of dollars immediately, it's a failure. This is a fundamental misunderstanding of how businesses actually grow.

Most highly profitable businesses take 1-2 years to hit meaningful cash flow. That's because the first few months—or even the first year—aren't about making money. They're about:

- **Figuring out what works**
- **Refining the business model**
- **Building an audience or customer base**

Take Mr. Beast, one of the highest-paid YouTubers in the world. For five years, his videos made zero money. But he kept experimenting, improving, and reinvesting—until suddenly, his audience exploded, and he was earning millions per month.

Or consider Steve Chou, a digital entrepreneur who started an e-commerce business with his wife selling handkerchiefs. For six months, they barely made sales. But once they optimized their marketing strategy, they were soon making over $100,000 per month.

Side hustles that don't make money immediately are often the most valuable—because they're the ones you've had time to refine properly.

Myth #4: "I need a unique idea"

A common belief is that profitable businesses require innovation. People think they need a game-changing idea—something the world has never seen before. In reality, the most successful businesses aren't original—they're just executed better.

Consider drop shipping, where people sell products without ever touching inventory. It's not new—it's a business model that has been around for decades. Yet thousands of entrepreneurs make six-figure incomes every year simply because they market and operate better than their competitors.

Look at content creators—many top YouTubers, writers, and influencers aren't doing anything groundbreaking. They're just delivering familiar content in a fresh, engaging way.

If you look at successful side hustlers, most of them didn't invent anything. They just:

- **Found a proven model** (freelancing, reselling, consulting).
- **Executed it consistently.**

Don't look for a perfect, unique idea. Look for something that works—and do it better.

Most people who never start a side hustle aren't lacking opportunity—they're just believing the wrong things.

- **You don't need a lot of money.**
- **You don't need to quit your job.**
- **You don't need overnight success.**
- **You don't need a "million-dollar idea."**

The real formula for building a successful side hustle? Start small. Execute consistently. Adjust based on results. Scale when ready.

Now that we've dismantled these myths, the real question is: How do you find the right side hustle for you? That's what we'll tackle in the next section.

Comparison of Traditional vs. Alternative Wealth-Building Strategies

One of the most common financial dilemmas people face is deciding between traditional wealth-building paths and alternative strategies that offer more flexibility, risk, and potential upside. While traditional methods provide stability and structure, alternative strategies often prioritize growth, autonomy, and income diversification.

Here's a clear comparison between the two approaches:

Traditional Wealth-Building	Alternative Wealth-Building
Corporate career & salary growth – Climbing the corporate ladder, earning a steady paycheck, and relying on incremental raises and promotions.	**Entrepreneurship & side hustles** – Building multiple income streams through freelancing, small businesses, or online ventures.
Employer-sponsored retirement plans (RRSP, 401(k), pensions) – Relying on employer contributions and long-term stock market growth.	**Self-directed investing & alternative assets** – Managing your own portfolio, investing in REITs, private equity, or startups.
Homeownership as a primary asset – Buying a home, building equity, and eventually selling at a profit.	**Real estate investments** – Generating cash flow through rental properties, short-term rentals, and real estate investment trusts (REITs).
Stock market investments – Long-term investing in index funds, ETFs, and dividend stocks for wealth accumulation.	**Alternative investments** – Exploring cryptocurrencies, collectibles, peer-to-peer lending, and private markets.

Linear wealth accumulation – Earning, saving, and growing assets steadily over decades.	**Exponential wealth-building** – Leveraging compounding, passive income, and scalable business models for faster financial independence.

While traditional methods offer predictability and lower risk, alternative strategies provide greater upside and independence—but often require more hands-on management and tolerance for uncertainty.

Finding the Right Side Hustle – The Profitability Formula

When most people think about starting a side hustle, their instinct is to ask themselves: *What am I passionate about?* It's a noble question, but a deeply flawed one. Passion is a terrible starting point for building a business. The world isn't short on passionate people—it's short on people who understand how to turn skills into income.

A better question would be: *What am I already good at that other people would pay for?* If you can answer that, you have the foundation for a profitable side hustle.

Take Vanessa, a Toronto-based marketing consultant who stumbled into her business completely by accident. She had spent years working for a corporate agency, handling SEO for large companies, but had never considered freelancing. One day, a family friend—a local gym owner—asked her if she could help them rank higher on Google. She charged a modest $500/month and helped them go from invisible to one of the top-ranked gyms in the city. Then, the gym referred her to a chiropractor. Then, another local business. Within a year, she was making $10,000 per month on the side—not because she was the most qualified SEO expert in Toronto, but because she was the first person in her network offering a valuable service.

The lesson? Side hustles don't require genius, innovation, or luck. They require finding a problem that people already want solved and becoming the person who can solve it.

A good side hustle isn't just about what you enjoy—it's about what works financially. Before jumping into a business, ask yourself:

1. **Low Startup Cost** – Does this require significant upfront capital? The best side hustles start lean. Avoid anything that forces you to sink thousands into inventory, rent, or advertising before you've made your first dollar.
2. **Predictable Cash Flow** – How quickly can you get paid? Service businesses, freelancing, and digital products generate immediate income, whereas businesses that require physical inventory often take months to become profitable.
3. **Scalability** – Can this grow beyond just trading time for money? The most powerful side hustles evolve from one-on-one work to automated or passive income streams—courses, memberships, subscription models, or outsourced operations.

The Side Hustle Stages – From Extra Cash to Full Business

One of the biggest reasons people fail at side hustles is that they don't treat them like a progression. They either rush in too fast—spending months on a website before making a single sale—or they expect overnight success and quit when they don't see immediate profits.

Successful side hustles go through three clear phases, and each one has its own set of goals.

Phase 1: Testing (Months 1-6)

The first six months of any side hustle should be treated like a low-risk experiment. Your only job during this stage is to prove that people are willing to pay you for something—not to build the perfect brand, hire employees, or spend months developing a product.

The best way to start lean? Sell first, refine later.

Consider Daniel, a college student in Vancouver who made his first $1,000 in three weeks—not by starting a formal business, but by offering resume-writing services on LinkedIn. He didn't launch a website, register an LLC, or print business cards. He just posted about his expertise, charged $50 per resume, and had his first paying customers within hours.

The biggest mistake most beginners make? *"Overbuilding before selling."* They invest time in designing the perfect logo, creating a fancy website, or mapping out a five-year growth plan—before ever testing whether anyone wants what they're selling.

During this phase, your first milestone is simple:
Make your first $1,000 as fast as possible.

The moment you earn money, you prove that your side hustle isn't just a hobby—it's an income stream.

Phase 2: Optimization (Months 6-18)

Once you've made your first few thousand dollars, the next step is turning your side hustle into a predictable, repeatable business. This phase is about efficiency—making more money without working more hours.

The first step? Raise your rates.

Most new side hustlers undervalue their work, charging prices that make growth impossible. If you're a freelancer charging $20 per hour, you'll burn out before ever hitting real income levels. The solution? Focus on results, not hours.

This is what Vanessa, the Toronto SEO consultant, did to increase her income tenfold. Instead of continuing to charge $500/month per client, she repositioned herself as a high-end specialist—charging $2,500/month, working with fewer clients, and making more money while working fewer hours.

Automate repetitive tasks.

- Use **Zapier** to automate emails and customer follow-ups.
- Use **Fiverr or Upwork** to outsource basic work to freelancers.
- Use **Canva, Notion, or Google Docs** to create repeatable templates.

Finally, many side hustlers transition from freelancing to productization. Instead of trading time for money, they create scalable offers—like a coach who starts selling courses instead of just one-on-one sessions, or a writer who turns their expertise into a paid newsletter or digital product.

At this stage, the biggest shift is from working harder to working smarter.

Phase 3: Scaling (Months 18+)

By the 18-month mark, a successful side hustle has two potential futures:

1. **It remains a side income**—bringing in $1,000–$5,000/month without requiring full-time effort.
2. **It becomes a full-fledged business**—scaling past six figures and replacing your salary.

The difference? Whether or not you've removed yourself from daily operations.

This is where automation, delegation, and passive income come into play. Instead of handling every transaction manually, successful hustlers scale by:

- **Hiring a virtual assistant** to handle admin work.
- **Building a team of freelancers** to deliver services.
- **Creating automated income streams** (subscriptions, digital products, memberships).

Take Steve, a former teacher who started a small business selling educational worksheets. For months, he spent hours per week writing new materials. But once he bundled his best worksheets into a digital course and sold them on Teachers Pay Teachers, his income tripled overnight—because he no longer had to create everything from scratch.

The most valuable businesses aren't just profitable—they're independent of the founder's daily effort.

At this point, the side hustle is no longer just extra income—it's an asset. Something that runs itself, generates revenue in the background, and provides true financial leverage.

Balancing a Side Hustle with a Full-Time Job

There's a common belief that running a side hustle alongside a full-time job means working 80-hour weeks, sacrificing sleep, and eventually burning out. This is why so many people hesitate—they assume that making extra money means trading all their free time for it. But the real secret of successful side hustlers? They don't work harder. They work smarter.

Consider Natalie, a Canadian elementary school teacher who always loved creating lesson plans. Like most educators, she wasn't making a fortune from her salary alone, but she had never considered monetizing her teaching materials—after all, lesson planning was just part of her job. But one evening, she stumbled upon Teachers Pay Teachers, an online marketplace where educators sell their worksheets and curriculum materials. Out of curiosity, she uploaded a few of her best lesson plans and priced them at $5 each. She expected nothing.

A week later, she checked her account—she had already made $250. Within six months, she was earning $2,500/month from selling materials she had already created for her own students. She never quit her job. She never worked crazy hours. She simply leveraged what she was already doing.

This is where most people get it wrong about side hustles. They assume they need to start something entirely new—learn a new skill, build a complex business, or work until exhaustion. The best side hustles, however, are built on existing skills, efficient systems, and strategic time management.

The 80/20 Rule

The biggest mistake new side hustlers make is spending time on things that don't make them money. They build a fancy website, design a logo, or endlessly tweak their Instagram page—before ever making a single sale.

The 80/20 Rule (Pareto Principle) states that 80% of your results come from just 20% of your efforts. When applied to a side hustle, this means:

- **Spending 80% of your time on activities that directly make you money**—finding clients, selling products, delivering services.
- **Spending only 20% of your time on secondary tasks**—branding, administration, or social media.

If you have limited time, you must prioritize income-producing actions. If you're a freelancer, that means finding paying clients, not redesigning your website. If you're selling digital products, that means launching them now—not perfecting every tiny detail before getting started.

The 10-Hour Rule

People assume that building a successful side hustle requires dozens of hours per week. But, data shows that most profitable side businesses take just 10 focused hours per week to generate a sustainable second income.

Here's why:

1. **Most businesses are built in short, focused time blocks**—not long, unstructured hours.
2. **If you spend those 10 hours efficiently, focusing on revenue-generating tasks**, you can make real progress.

For example, let's say you have just 10 hours per week to work on a side hustle:

- **3 hours** finding and interacting with potential clients/customers.
- **5 hours** delivering the actual work or creating products.
- **2 hours** automating processes or optimizing the business.

If you stick to this schedule, you could easily generate $1,000 to $2,000/month within a few months—without working crazy hours.

Avoiding Burnout - Not Every Side Hustle Needs to Be Full-Time

Another misconception is that every side hustle needs to turn into a massive business. But sometimes, a small, steady side income is enough.

- A side hustle making **$500/month** covers a car payment.
- A **$1,500/month** side business could fund a mortgage.
- A **$3,000/month** hustle gives you financial security if you ever lose your job.

Not everyone needs to quit their job and become an entrepreneur. Sometimes, the best side hustle is simply one that removes financial stress.

Managing Money Like an Entrepreneur

Most people who start side hustles never actually build wealth from them. They get caught in a cycle—making money, reinvesting everything, and never actually seeing financial progress. They don't manage their money like an entrepreneur.

Mistake #1: Not Separating Personal and Business Finances

Many side hustlers mistakenly mix personal and business finances. They get paid into their personal bank account, spend the money however they like, and at the end of the month, they have no idea how much they actually earned.

Create a separate bank account for your side hustle. Even if you're just making $500/month, treat it like a real business. When you separate income and expenses, you instantly become more strategic about where your money is going.

Mistake #2: Reinvesting Every Dollar Instead of Taking Profits

A surprising number of new side hustlers make money and immediately spend it on "growth." They buy better software, upgrade their website, or pay for expensive courses—without ever actually paying themselves.

Rule of thumb: Always take a percentage of your earnings as personal profit.

- **First $1,000?** Keep at least **50% as cash in your pocket** before reinvesting.
- **Making $2,000/month?** Pay yourself a **fixed salary** before spending on anything else.

The goal of a side hustle isn't just to reinvest endlessly—it's to improve your financial position right now.

Mistake #3: Forgetting About Taxes—And Overpaying as a Result

Most first-time entrepreneurs forget about taxes until it's too late. In both Canada and the U.S., self-employed income isn't automatically taxed—which means many new side hustlers suddenly owe thousands of dollars at tax time.

Plan for taxes in advance—and take advantage of deductions.

- **In Canada:**
  - You can deduct business expenses—software, travel, internet costs.
  - RRSP/TFSA strategies allow entrepreneurs to lower taxable income.
  - Incorporating (if making over $50,000/year) can reduce tax rates.
- **In the U.S.:**
  - LLCs and sole proprietors can write off expenses—laptops, software, workspace.
  - Home office deductions allow you to reduce taxable income.
  - Health insurance premiums can often be deducted as a business expense.

Managing money wisely means keeping more of what you earn—not just making more and watching it disappear.

"You don't need a business idea. You don't need a lot of money. You just need the ability to recognize opportunities and take action."

If a billion-dollar company like Airbnb started as a side hustle, what's stopping you from taking the first step?

Too many people overthink the process. They wait for perfect conditions, the perfect idea, the perfect timing. Meanwhile, others take small, imperfect actions—and end up building something meaningful.

Commit to launching something in 30 days.

- No perfect ideas.
- No excuses.
- Just **execution.**

Where do you start?

1. Pick a **skill you already have** that people would pay for.
2. Find **your first paying customer** within 30 days.
3. Optimize, refine, and **turn it into a real income stream.**

Side hustles aren't just about money—they're about control, security, and freedom.

HOW TO KEEP YOUR
FINANCES IN PEAK
CONDITION

Chapter 15 - Why Most People Lose Wealth Faster Than They Earn It

Mike Tyson once had it all—a fortune exceeding $400 million, an empire built on sheer dominance in the ring, and a life of extravagance that seemed untouchable. Yet, within a few short years, it was all gone. The same fists that had earned him more money than most people could fathom were now clenched in frustration as he stood before a bankruptcy judge. He wasn't alone. Over 70% of professional athletes go broke within five years of retirement, and their financial downfalls are as predictable as they are preventable.

It's easy to look at Tyson's downfall and think, *That could never happen to me. I'm not buying tigers or gold-plated bathtubs.* But the truth is, his mistake was not an exception—it was an amplified version of what most high earners do on a smaller scale. His millions disappeared due to the same factors that cause middle-class professionals to end up in financial trouble:

- **Overestimating future income**
- **Failing to control spending despite rising earnings**
- **Making investments they didn't understand**
- **Not preparing for financial downturns**

The shocking reality is that making money is not the hard part. Keeping it is. If it were simply a matter of earning more, then high-income professionals, lottery winners, and world-class athletes would never go broke. But time and time again, they do.

For a more relatable example, let's look at Ryan, a Canadian tech entrepreneur from Vancouver. By 35, he had successfully sold his first startup for a life-changing $4.5 million. It wasn't enough to retire forever, but it was a solid foundation for financial security. He knew he had to be smart with the money, so he did what many people in his position do—he hired a financial advisor, diversified his investments, and set aside a chunk for long-term savings.

But as his wealth grew, so did his spending. A waterfront condo in Vancouver ($2.3 million). A Tesla Model X ($150,000). Frequent business-class flights, designer suits, a few angel investments in "promising" startups. He wasn't being reckless—he was just living a life that "matched" his newfound success.

Then came the market crash of 2022. A few of his investments tanked. His startup funding dried up. He wasn't technically bankrupt, but his liquidity disappeared overnight. Within three years of selling his company, Ryan was nearly back where he started, except now with a mortgage and fixed expenses that required a high income to sustain.

His mistake wasn't making bad money decisions—it was assuming that he had made it. That once wealth was built, it was permanent. But money doesn't work that way. It has to be managed, protected, and constantly adjusted to new conditions.

Why Most People Who Earn Well Never Build Wealth

The common theme in these stories isn't stupidity—it's financial fragility. Most people, regardless of income level, operate under the illusion of financial permanence:

- **They assume that their peak earnings will last forever.**

- **They believe a high salary equals financial security.**
- **They increase their lifestyle costs as fast as their income grows.**
- **They don't protect against the inevitable downturns.**

The truth is, financial security isn't about how much you make—it's about how much you keep and how well you manage risk.

So, if making money isn't the hard part, what is?

It's holding onto it and making it last.

The irony of financial success is that the skill set needed to build wealth is different from the one required to keep it. Earning money is about work ethic, skills, and opportunity. But preserving wealth? That requires:

- **A deep understanding of financial risks.**
- **A system for managing income and investments without lifestyle creep.**
- **The discipline to protect wealth from bad investments and overleveraging.**

If financial stability is the goal, then thinking like an investor—not just an earner—is the key.

The 3 Biggest Money Lies That Keep People Broke

Most people are operating under outdated financial beliefs—ideas that were once true but no longer work in today's economy. These myths prevent high earners from actually becoming financially independent.

Myth 1: "A High Income Means You'll Always Be Fine"

People assume that as long as they **earn enough money**, they'll be set. But history says otherwise:

- 60% of NBA and NHL players go bankrupt within 5 years of retirement.
- 1 in 3 lottery winners **lose everything** within a decade.
- Even doctors and lawyers—two of the highest-paid professions—often struggle financially due to debt and poor money management.

A high income is like a speeding car—it can take you far, but without brakes (financial systems), you'll eventually crash.

Myth 2: "Owning Assets = Financial Security"

Owning a house, a luxury car, or a successful business might look like financial success—but assets don't guarantee security if they aren't producing cash flow.

Ryan, the tech entrepreneur from Vancouver, had millions in assets, but none of them were liquid when he needed them. Tyson had mansions and exotic pets, but they were liabilities, not wealth-building vehicles.

The real question isn't how much you own—it's how much your assets work for you.

- A **rental property** that generates passive income? Smart.
- A **luxury home** that requires $15,000/month in mortgage payments? A ticking time bomb.
- A **business that can operate without you?** Freedom.
- A **business that collapses if you step away?** A disguised job.

Assets should be income-generating or low-maintenance. Otherwise, they aren't wealth—they're expenses disguised as investments.

Myth 3: "More Investments = More Wealth"

Some people believe the answer to staying wealthy is investing aggressively—buying real estate, stocks, businesses, crypto, startups. But without strategy, investing can be just as dangerous as reckless spending.

- **Most tech startups fail.**
- **Real estate can be risky in market downturns.**
- **Day trading creates more losers than winners.**

Instead of blindly investing in everything, the wealthy follow one simple rule:

The goal isn't to maximize returns—it's to maximize financial resilience. Building wealth is about taking smart risks. Staying wealthy is about avoiding dumb ones.

Mike Tyson didn't go broke because he stopped making money—he went broke because he never adjusted to financial reality. Ryan, the tech entrepreneur didn't fail because of one bad decision—he failed because he assumed his high-income lifestyle was sustainable forever.

The truth is, no amount of income can outpace bad financial habits. The only way to achieve true financial security is by shifting from an income mindset to a wealth-preservation mindset.

The Regular Financial Check-Up—The Most Overlooked Wealth Strategy

Most people treat financial planning as a one-time event. They assume that once they have a high salary, a well-diversified investment portfolio, and a comfortable savings buffer, their financial future is set. But this mindset is like believing that going to the gym once guarantees lifelong fitness or that changing the oil in your car once means you'll never have engine trouble. Just as health, career, and relationships require ongoing care, so does financial well-being.

Yet, if you ask the average high earner when they last reviewed their investments, updated their budget, or reassessed their financial goals, you'll likely be met with silence or a vague answer. People are diligent about getting annual physicals, car tune-ups, and home inspections—but when it comes to money, most assume they can "set and forget" their financial plan. That assumption is dangerous.

The wealthiest individuals don't become (or stay) rich by accident. They conduct regular financial audits, adjust to new circumstances, and stay ahead of economic changes. A financial plan that made sense five years ago might be completely outdated today due to inflation, market downturns, tax law changes, or shifts in personal priorities.

Ignoring your finances doesn't just slow down wealth-building—it can actively erode it. The real risk isn't just failing to make more money. It's failing to keep what you already have.

How to Conduct a Wealth Check-Up

Think of this as your annual financial physical. Just as a doctor checks your vital signs, a wealth check-up examines the key indicators of financial health and identifies where adjustments are needed.

Step 1: Review Your Net Worth Quarterly

Your net worth is your **financial pulse.** It's the most straightforward measure of whether you are actually building wealth or just spinning your wheels.

- **Net worth formula:** Assets (cash, real estate, investments) – Liabilities (debts, mortgages, loans).
- If your net worth is **growing**, you're on track. If it's **shrinking**, lifestyle creep or bad investments could be eating into your gains.
- Tracking your net worth over time reveals patterns. **Are you wealthier today than you were last year? If not, why?**

Many people assume they're financially successful because they make six or seven figures. But net worth is a far better indicator of wealth than income. A $500,000 salary means nothing if expenses outpace it.

Step 2: Analyze Cash Flow

A high salary can disguise poor money management. Just because money is coming in doesn't mean it's being put to good use.

- **How much of your income is actually saved or invested?**
- **Are your expenses increasing faster than your earnings?**

- **Are you spending money on things that contribute to your financial future—or just making payments on depreciating assets?**

One of the most effective wealth-building habits is the **50/30/20 rule**:

- **50% needs** (housing, bills, essentials)
- **30% wants** (lifestyle, entertainment, discretionary spending)
- **20% wealth-building** (investments, savings, debt reduction)

But here's the secret: The wealthiest people flip this ratio. They don't save 20%—they save 50% and live off the rest. The question isn't how much you earn but how much of it stays in your possession.

Step 3: Assess Investment Allocations

If you set up an investment portfolio five years ago and haven't checked it since, it's probably not serving you as well as it could. Markets shift, tax laws change, and economic conditions evolve.

- **Are your investments still aligned with your risk tolerance?**
- **Has the market created new opportunities you're missing?**
- **Are you rebalancing your portfolio, or are you overexposed to risk?**

Most people overestimate their risk tolerance when markets are booming. They think, *I can handle volatility*—until the market crashes, and they panic-sell at the worst possible time.

A disciplined investor reviews their portfolio regularly and adjusts based on strategy, not emotion.

Step 4: Revisit Financial Goals

Five years ago, you might have wanted a vacation home. Now, you might prefer to retire early. Your goals change, but if your financial plan doesn't evolve with them, you'll drift in the wrong direction.

- **Are you still on track for retirement at your desired age?**
- **Do your savings support the lifestyle you want?**
- **Have family, career, or personal priorities shifted?**

Money is a tool. The question isn't just how much you have, but whether it's helping you achieve what matters most.

Step 5: Prepare for Economic Uncertainty

The most financially secure people aren't the ones who predict the future correctly. They're the ones who are prepared for any outcome.

- **Emergency Fund:** Do you have at least **6-12 months of cash reserves** to cover expenses if your income stopped tomorrow?
- **Tax-Advantaged Accounts:** Are you **maximizing contributions to RRSPs, TFSAs (Canada) or 401(k)s, IRAs (U.S.)**?
- **Inflation Hedge:** Are you investing in assets that can keep pace with inflation—such as real estate, stocks, or inflation-protected bonds?

The key isn't just making more money—it's protecting what you have from unexpected economic shifts. Financial health isn't a one-time achievement. It's a routine process. The wealthiest people don't "set and forget"—they audit and adjust.

The Wealth Preservation Mindset—Why You Must Protect Before You Grow

Making money is only half the game. The real challenge is keeping it.

Most people believe the solution to financial stress is earning more. They think that if they could just make an extra $50,000 or $100,000 a year, their problems would disappear.

But the truth is, a bigger paycheck won't fix poor money habits.

The Biggest Wealth-Killing Mistakes

1. **Lifestyle Inflation -** As income grows, so does spending. New house. New car. More expensive vacations. Suddenly, your monthly costs match (or exceed) your increased earnings. The difference between rich and wealthy is simple: *Rich people make a lot. Wealthy people keep a lot.*

2. **Over-Leveraging Assets -** Real estate and business expansion are great—until **debt outpaces cash flow.** Borrowing money isn't inherently bad, but it becomes dangerous when:

    - You rely on rising markets to sustain investments.
    - You have no liquidity to cover downturns.
    - Your entire net worth is tied up in illiquid assets.

3. **Chasing High-Risk Investments -** Doctors, engineers, and executives—high-income professionals—often fall into the trap of investing in what they don't understand. They assume they need to "keep up" with crypto traders, stock speculators, or risky startups.

But, the most successful investors prioritize consistency over hype.

Continual Learning & Financial Adaptation

Money doesn't keep itself. The financial landscape shifts constantly—tax laws change, markets fluctuate, new asset classes emerge—and failing to keep up is like running a business without ever checking your revenue or expenses. You can't rely on a single financial playbook for life. The moment you assume you know everything about money is the moment you start falling behind.

Most people don't go broke because they *don't earn enough*. They go broke because they fail to adapt to new financial realities. They treat their past financial successes as a guarantee of future security, forgetting that what worked five years ago might be completely outdated today. Financial success is an ongoing process—one that rewards those who stay informed, update their strategies, and embrace financial learning as a lifelong habit.

Think about the past decade. The financial landscape is unrecognizable compared to ten years ago.

- **2010s:** Interest rates were at historic lows. Mortgage rates in Canada and the U.S. hovered around **2-3%**, making real estate a goldmine. Borrowing was cheap, and many homeowners locked in decades-long, ultra-low fixed rates.
- **2020s:** Inflation soared. The Bank of Canada and the U.S. Federal Reserve aggressively raised rates. Mortgage renewals are now **double or triple what they were in 2020**, crushing homeowners who didn't plan ahead.

- **2010s:** The traditional 60/40 portfolio (60% stocks, 40% bonds) was the go-to investment strategy. It provided steady returns and reliable income.
- **2020s:** Bonds are struggling, inflation is eating into returns, and alternative investments (real estate, private equity, even cryptocurrency) are becoming necessary for diversification.
- **2010s:** Side hustles were rare.
- **2020s:** The **gig economy exploded**, offering opportunities for extra income—but also new tax and financial planning complexities.

The rules of financial success are always evolving. The wealthiest individuals don't just *make money*—they stay ahead of financial trends, anticipate risks, and adjust their strategies accordingly.

How to Stay Financially Educated Without Overwhelm

Most people assume that staying financially educated means reading a mountain of investment books, memorizing tax codes, and following every finance headline. That's not sustainable. The goal isn't to drown in financial information—it's to focus on the right sources and build a system for lifelong learning.

Step 1: Follow Trusted Financial Experts & Sources

Not all financial advice is equal. The internet is flooded with so-called "experts" pushing bad investment advice, get-rich-quick schemes, or overly complicated strategies. The key is to curate a handful of high-quality sources and stick with them.

- **The Motley Fool** – Clear, research-backed investment advice for long-term investors.

- **Bloomberg Wealth** – A mix of macroeconomic insights, personal finance trends, and market news.
- **Ramit Sethi** – Author of *I Will Teach You to Be Rich*, he focuses on automation and psychology-driven financial strategies.
- **Wealthsimple Magazine** – Provides insights into investing, taxes, and long-term financial planning in a Canadian context.
- **The Globe and Mail's Financial Section** – A great resource for Canadian stock market trends and economic policy updates.
- **Preet Banerjee** – A Canadian personal finance expert known for making complex financial topics digestible.

Step 2: Engage in Practical Learning

Most people try to learn about finance passively—they watch YouTube videos, read blogs, or listen to financial podcasts. But real financial knowledge comes from taking action. You wouldn't learn to swim by watching someone else do it—you have to jump in the water.

Three ways to learn by doing:

1. **Investment Simulations**
    - If you're hesitant to invest, start with **mock portfolios**. Platforms like Investopedia's simulator or Wealthsimple's practice mode allow you to **test strategies in real-world conditions—without risking real money**.
    - Experiment with different asset allocations. Learn how **market movements impact different investments**.
2. **Budgeting Challenges**
    - Challenge yourself to **cut 10% of your expenses for one month**—and reinvest that amount.

    - Try a **“no-spend” week**—forcing you to rethink habitual spending.
    - Track **every dollar you spend for 30 days**. The simple act of awareness can trigger major financial behavior changes.
3. **Hands-On Money Management**
    - Instead of letting financial advisors or automated systems handle everything, **force yourself to manually track** one aspect of your finances—whether it’s net worth, investment contributions, or a new revenue stream.
    - **The more hands-on you are, the more you understand the mechanics of wealth-building.**

Step 3: Get Professional Advice When Needed

Even the most financially savvy individuals don’t do everything alone. At some point, you’ll hit a complexity threshold—whether it’s estate planning, tax optimization, or structuring business income. Knowing when to bring in a financial professional can save you money in the long run.

- **Hire a fee-only financial planner** – Avoids conflicts of interest since they **don’t earn commissions on products they sell**.
- **Consult an accountant for tax efficiency** – The tax code changes constantly. A good accountant can **save you thousands through deductions and tax-advantaged accounts**.
- **Ensure your estate plan is up to date** – A will and proper estate planning can prevent **legal battles, excessive taxes, and lost wealth upon inheritance**.

You don't need a financial advisor to tell you how to budget or avoid debt, but when you're making complex wealth decisions, expert guidance is invaluable.

This chapter started with a reality check: Staying wealthy is harder than getting wealthy. The people who thrive financially for decades aren't the smartest or the highest earners—they're the ones who build financial resilience.

We've broken down the four pillars of financial longevity:

1. **Regular financial check-ups** keep your money aligned with your life goals.
2. **Wealth preservation strategies** prevent common pitfalls like lifestyle inflation, overleveraging, and bad investments.
3. **Continual learning and adaptation** ensure you don't fall behind as financial trends evolve.
4. **Financial resilience and planning for uncertainty** secure your wealth against unpredictable life events.

Most people focus only on making money. The financially successful focus on keeping, growing, and protecting it over decades.

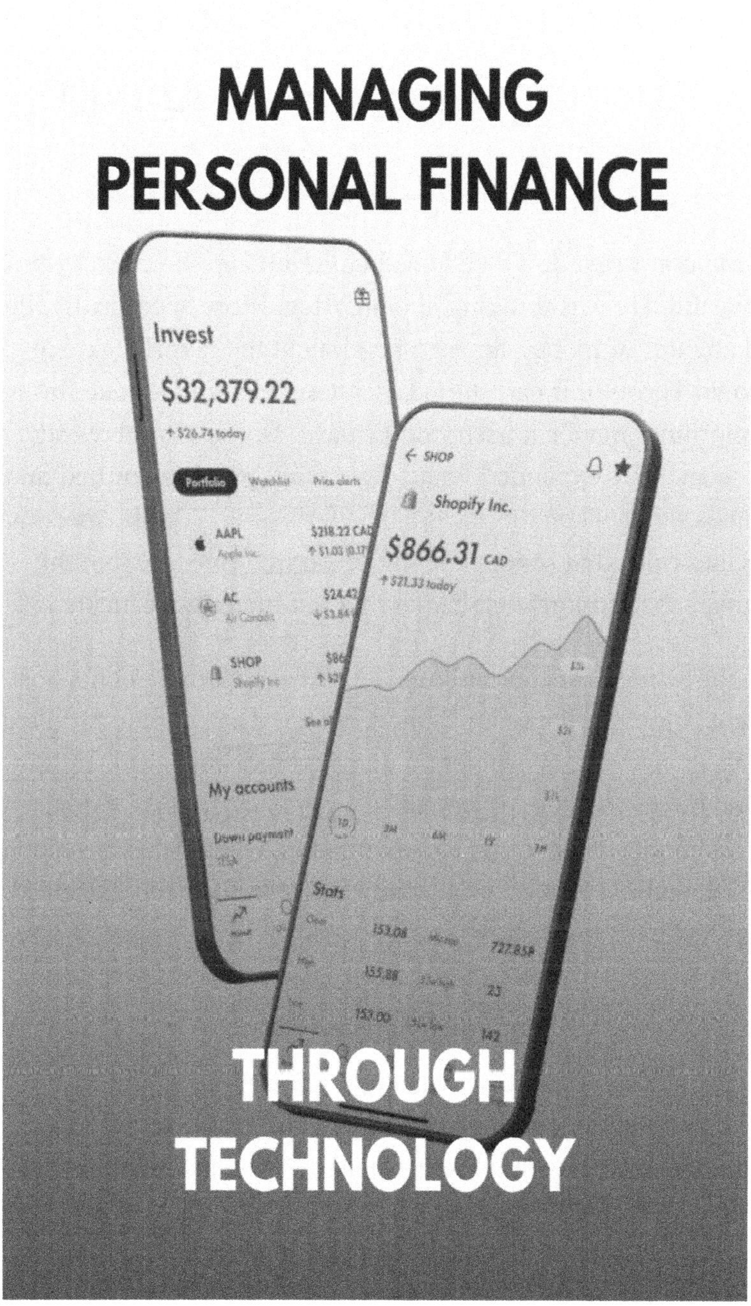
MANAGING
PERSONAL FINANCE
Invest
$32,379.22
Portfolio
AAPL
SHOP
My accounts
← SHOP
Shopify Inc.
$866.31 CAD
Stats
THROUGH
TECHNOLOGY

Chapter 16 - How to Use Automation to Stay Ahead

When Malcolm first downloaded a budgeting app, he wasn't thinking about wealth. He was thinking about coffee. More specifically, the absurd amount of money he was spending at his favorite café in downtown Toronto. It had started as a harmless ritual—one flat white in the morning, maybe a pastry on Fridays. But as his career advanced and his social life expanded, that single daily purchase turned into two, sometimes three. Then there were the "let's grab a drink" meetings, the quick Uber rides that seemed negligible at the time, the monthly streaming subscriptions that he barely used but never canceled.

One night, while scrolling through Twitter, he stumbled on a post from a financial blogger that read: "You don't have a spending problem—you have an awareness problem." The next morning, still slightly unsettled by the idea, he downloaded a personal finance app just to see where his money was going. He assumed he was relatively responsible with his spending. After all, he made six figures in tech. He wasn't reckless—he was just living his life.

The app told a different story.

In the first month of tracking, Malcolm realized he was spending over $1,200 on discretionary purchases he couldn't even recall making. What surprised him even more was that, despite his high income, he was barely saving. The numbers didn't add up. How was it possible to make good money and still feel like financial security was always slightly out of reach?

That was when Malcolm's curiosity turned into a habit. He started exploring beyond the budgeting app, discovering automated savings tools, robo-advisors, tax optimization software, and debt management algorithms that made decisions for him—decisions he previously assumed required discipline, spreadsheets, and hours of financial planning. Five years later, Malcolm wasn't just spending less on coffee. He had built a six-figure investment portfolio, maxed out his tax-advantaged accounts, and saved thousands in tax deductions—all without hiring a financial advisor or making radical lifestyle changes.

Financial success was no longer about willpower. Technology had leveled the playing field, automating the same wealth-building strategies that were once only available to the ultra-rich.

From Passive Tracking to Active Financial Optimization

Most people think of financial apps as passive tools—ways to track spending, set budgets, or monitor net worth. They log in when they feel guilty about a large purchase or when they get a bank notification about an upcoming bill. But this approach to technology is like owning a gym membership but never showing up to lift weights. The real benefits come when these tools move from passive tracking to active financial optimization—when they don't just record financial decisions but actively improve them.

It wasn't always this way. A decade ago, the most people could do with financial technology was check their account balances and categorize expenses manually. Today, AI-powered platforms can:

- **Analyze spending patterns** and suggest automatic adjustments.
- **Optimize savings contributions** based on real-time income and expenses.
- **Invest money intelligently** based on personal risk tolerance and market conditions.
- **Minimize tax burdens** by automatically identifying deductions most people overlook.

Those who truly benefit from financial technology aren't just using apps—they are outsourcing financial decision-making to data-driven systems. They are letting algorithms do the heavy lifting, much like a hedge fund manager would for their clients.

Take two people, both earning $75,000 a year. The first person downloads a budgeting app, checks it occasionally, and tries to cut spending where possible. The second person integrates a full ecosystem of financial technology:

- A **robo-advisor** that automatically invests and rebalances based on market conditions.
- **Automated tax optimization tools** that reduce taxable income and increase investment returns.
- **Smart savings features** that round up transactions and deposit the difference into high-interest accounts.

At the end of five years, their incomes are the same, but their financial futures look entirely different. The first person is financially stable. The second person has built actual wealth.

This is where most people get it wrong: they assume financial security is about earning more money. But in reality, it's about optimizing the money you already have.

Why Convenience is the Wrong Goal

One of the biggest mistakes people make when using financial technology is assuming that it's just about making money management more convenient. This is a dangerously limited perspective.

Technology is not just about saving time—it's about compounding advantages over time. A person who uses a budgeting app may find it easier to track their spending. A person who uses AI-powered investing and tax automation is building wealth without thinking about it. The difference is exponential.

Consider the case of someone earning $100,000 a year. Without any automation, they might save 10% of their income by manually moving money into savings accounts and retirement funds. But with financial automation, that same person could:

- **Save 20-30% of their income** because their savings and investments are deducted before they even see their paycheck.
- **Reduce taxable income** through tax-loss harvesting strategies built into their investment platform.
- **Eliminate wasted expenses** by using machine learning to analyze subscription services, utility costs, and discretionary spending.

Over 10 years, the difference between these two people is millions of dollars.

The problem is that most people underestimate the power of automation. They assume that financial success is about willpower, discipline, and making the right choices every day. But the truth is that people who remove financial decisions from their daily routine end up wealthier than those who rely on self-control.

The best financial decisions are the ones that don't have to be made at all—because they were automated months or years ago.

How Smart Money Uses Technology for Wealth-Building

For decades, the wealthiest individuals had access to financial advantages the average person simply couldn't touch. They had portfolio managers who rebalanced their investments daily, tax strategists who ensured they paid as little as legally possible, and debt structuring specialists who made sure they never carried the kind of high-interest burdens that quietly drained middle-class earners. The average person, on the other hand, was left to navigate the financial world largely on their own—relying on gut instinct, generic advice, and whatever they could piece together from news articles or personal finance books.

But that is no longer the case.

The most significant shift in personal finance over the last decade isn't just the rise of new investment platforms, digital banking, or automated savings tools. It's the fact that technology has democratized wealth-building strategies that were once reserved for the ultra-rich. Today, anyone with a smartphone and an internet connection has access to sophisticated financial tools that automate, optimize, and execute wealth-building decisions—often more efficiently than a human could.

The real dividing line is no longer between the rich and the poor or even between high earners and low earners. It is between those who leverage financial technology to accelerate wealth-building and those who continue to manage their money manually, missing out on advantages that could change their financial trajectory.

Automated Investing: The New Wealth Manager

Once upon a time, investing was a privilege reserved for those who either had the expertise to navigate financial markets or the wealth to pay for professional advice. If you wanted a well-diversified portfolio tailored to your risk tolerance and financial goals, you had to hire a financial advisor—someone who would charge hefty management fees, typically 1-2% of assets under management, on top of commissions and fund expense ratios. These fees might not seem significant, but over time, they could erode tens, even hundreds of thousands of dollars in potential investment returns.

Then came robo-advisors, and everything changed.

Platforms like Wealthsimple in Canada and Betterment in the U.S. introduced a radical idea: what if investment management could be handled not by humans, but by algorithms? What if, instead of hiring a financial planner, an individual could simply enter their income, savings goals, and risk tolerance into an app, and have an AI-powered system construct and manage their portfolio for a fraction of the cost?

The technology works by automatically balancing portfolios using a mix of low-cost exchange-traded funds (ETFs), optimizing asset allocations based on market conditions, and minimizing tax burdens through strategies like tax-loss harvesting. It is, in essence, an elite wealth management strategy—without the elite fees.

Consider the financial impact of two individuals who both invest $10,000 per year for 30 years. One chooses a traditional financial advisor, charging 1.5% annually, while the other uses a robo-advisor with a 0.25% fee. Assuming an average market return of 7%, the difference in portfolio value at the end of 30 years is staggering: the individual with the traditional advisor ends up with approximately $790,000, while the one using a robo-advisor accumulates over $1.1 million—a difference of over $300,000, simply due to lower fees.

The lesson here is clear: access to investing is no longer the problem—costly inefficiencies are.

Robo-advisors provide automated wealth-building strategies that require no market expertise and cost a fraction of traditional financial services. Those who still believe investing requires picking stocks or paying for expensive advice are operating on an outdated model that benefits financial institutions far more than individuals.

Debt Repayment Optimization: Outsmarting Interest

If investing is the fastest way to build wealth, debt is the fastest way to destroy it.

Most people assume that debt is a function of poor financial decisions—overspending, bad habits, or an inability to live within one's means. But in reality, the financial system is designed to keep people in debt.

The average person who carries a balance on their credit card isn't paying just the listed interest rate—they are often paying twice, sometimes three times the original cost of their purchases over time. The reason? Minimum payments are engineered to keep borrowers trapped in a cycle of compounding interest.

The traditional approach to paying off debt has always been painfully inefficient. People either pay a little extra each month, hoping to make a dent, or they try the psychological trick of the snowball method—paying off smaller balances first to build momentum. But neither of these strategies is truly optimized for wealth preservation.

This is where debt repayment algorithms have changed the game.

Apps like Tally (U.S.) and similar automated debt management tools take over the repayment process entirely, analyzing outstanding debts, consolidating balances at lower interest rates, and creating an optimized repayment schedule that minimizes total interest paid. Instead of relying on self-discipline to make extra payments, technology ensures that debt is repaid in the most mathematically efficient way possible.

Imagine two people with identical credit card debt—$15,000 spread across three cards at varying interest rates. One follows the traditional route, making slightly more than the minimum payments each month, which—if they only pay an extra $100 per month—could still take them over a decade to clear due to compounding interest. The other person uses a debt repayment app, consolidates the balances, and has their payments structured to eliminate high-interest debt first. Instead of 10+ years, they are debt-free in three to five years.

This is not a trivial difference. The first person will pay thousands of dollars in extra interest. The second will redirect that money toward investments, savings, or wealth-building activities.

Again, the takeaway is clear: the people who optimize financial technology to eliminate inefficient costs build wealth far faster than those who rely on outdated debt management strategies.

Tax Optimization: The Silent Wealth Multiplier

If there's one area where the wealthy have always outmaneuvered the average person, it is taxes.

For decades, high-net-worth individuals have structured their finances to minimize taxable income, defer tax payments, and maximize deductions—all legally. The problem? Most people assume these strategies require hiring accountants or tax attorneys.

They don't.

Today, AI-driven tax optimization tools allow everyday earners to use the same tax-saving strategies that the wealthy have relied on for generations. The difference between someone who pays the full tax burden on their income and someone who strategically reduces taxable income is not just a few hundred dollars—it is a difference measured in six or seven figures over a lifetime.

Consider how tax-efficient technology is being used in Canada and the U.S.:

- **Automated RRSP contributions (Canada) and 401(k) deferrals (U.S.)** reduce taxable income, lowering the total tax bill while building retirement wealth.
- **AI-driven tax software** automatically identifies deductions most people overlook, such as home office expenses, investment-related deductions, and education credits.
- **Tax-loss harvesting strategies** allow investors to offset capital gains with losing investments, reducing what they owe on investment income.

These strategies were once the domain of elite financial advisors. Today, they are embedded in personal finance apps and investment platforms available to anyone.

The biggest difference between those who build wealth and those who struggle financially is not just income—it's how well they optimize their financial decisions.

People who integrate technology into their investment, debt, and tax strategies are not just "managing money better." They are playing an entirely different financial game—one where technology works for them, not against them.

Those who fail to leverage these tools aren't just missing out on convenience. They are paying a financial penalty—one measured in lost wealth, missed opportunities, and unnecessary expenses.

The real question isn't whether financial technology can help people build wealth. It's whether they are willing to use it before it's too late.

The Automation Formula – How to Make Wealth-Building Effortless

For centuries, wealth accumulation was a matter of discipline and sheer willpower. People were told to save diligently, invest wisely, and avoid wasteful spending. Those who succeeded were often praised for their financial prudence, while those who failed were blamed for a lack of restraint. But this traditional view of money management is not just outdated—it is fundamentally flawed.

Technology has changed the game. The wealthiest individuals today are not necessarily the most disciplined, nor are they the ones constantly tracking every expense or researching every investment decision. Instead, they are the ones who have built systems that make financial success happen automatically. The difference between those who struggle financially and those who thrive is no longer just about earning more money—it's about leveraging automation to remove human error from wealth-building.

Consider two individuals with identical salaries. One saves sporadically, investing only when they "remember" to, paying bills manually, and monitoring spending through sheer willpower. The other automates everything—savings, investments, expenses, even financial protection. After ten years, the second person has accumulated far more wealth—not because they were smarter or worked harder, but because their financial system worked for them while they focused on other things.

This is the true advantage of financial technology: it removes the need for discipline.

There is a simple three-step formula that eliminates financial guesswork and ensures that wealth accumulates without constant effort:

Step 1: Automate Wealth Accumulation

Most people approach saving and investing backward. They spend first and save whatever is left over. But in reality, wealth is built by reversing this formula—saving first and spending what remains. The challenge, of course, is that this requires ongoing willpower. And willpower, as every behavioral economist will tell you, is finite.

This is why the wealthy don't rely on willpower—they rely on systems.

Automating wealth accumulation means setting up invisible, automatic transactions that move money into savings and investments before it even touches a checking account. This removes human emotion from financial decisions, eliminating the temptation to overspend.

One of the simplest and most effective ways to automate wealth-building is to set up recurring contributions to investment accounts. For example, in Canada, individuals can schedule automatic transfers to RRSPs (Registered Retirement Savings Plans) and TFSAs (Tax-Free Savings Accounts). In the U.S., the equivalent would be 401(k) contributions or automatic deposits into IRAs (Individual Retirement Accounts).

The power of automation becomes clear when looking at long-term results. A person who manually saves for retirement "when they remember to" might contribute inconsistently—some years maxing out contributions, other years forgetting entirely. Meanwhile, someone who sets up a recurring transfer of just $500 per month into an investment account will, after 30 years at a conservative 7% annual return, have accumulated over $600,000, all without having to think about it.

Even micro-savings automation—such as apps that round up everyday purchases and deposit the spare change into an investment account—can have a compounding effect over time. Wealth is rarely built in dramatic windfalls; it is accumulated through consistent, automatic systems that remove human inconsistency from the equation.

The ultimate goal is this: saving should feel effortless.

Step 2: Automate Expense Management

One of the biggest myths about financial success is that it requires meticulous budgeting. The conventional wisdom says that to stay financially healthy, people must track every dollar, analyze spending categories, and make careful adjustments each month. But in reality, very few wealthy individuals manually budget their money—because they don't need to.

Instead, they set automated limits and let technology do the work.

At its core, automating expense management means eliminating financial drift—the small, unconscious spending decisions that quietly drain wealth. This happens in three key ways:

First, by using financial apps that automatically categorize and track spending, individuals can monitor expenses without actively budgeting. The best tools don't just show transactions—they send real-time alerts when spending exceeds a preset threshold, allowing users to adjust before financial damage is done.

Second, automatic bill payments ensure that essential expenses are never missed, protecting credit scores and avoiding unnecessary late fees. A shocking number of high-income earners have suboptimal credit ratings, not because they lack money, but because they forget to pay bills on time. A single missed payment can result in a penalty, interest charges, and even a negative impact on a credit report. Automating all recurring payments eliminates this entirely.

Third, subscription management tools track and cancel unused services. The average person is subscribed to multiple digital services they no longer use—from streaming platforms to unused gym memberships. Companies thrive on the fact that people forget to cancel, quietly billing them month after month. But apps now exist that automatically scan bank statements, identify subscriptions, and even cancel unwanted charges with a single click.

By automating expense management, wealth-building stops being about financial micromanagement and instead becomes about financial efficiency. Those who automate their spending guardrails don't need to make perfect financial decisions every day—because the system they've set up prevents bad ones from happening.

Step 3: Automate Wealth Protection

Building wealth is only half the battle. Keeping it is just as important.

Many people assume that wealth preservation requires sophisticated financial knowledge—estate planning, tax strategies, or legal protections. But in reality, most wealth protection comes down to simple, automated actions that prevent catastrophic financial mistakes.

One of the most overlooked areas of financial automation is AI-powered insurance comparison tools. Most people renew insurance policies without shopping for better rates, assuming that premiums increase naturally over time. But in reality, insurance companies count on customer inertia—gradually increasing rates, knowing that most people won't bother switching.

AI-driven platforms now automatically shop for the best insurance rates, ensuring optimal coverage at the lowest cost without requiring any manual effort. Those who fail to use these tools often overpay hundreds or even thousands of dollars per year on unnecessary premiums.

Another critical area of wealth protection is credit monitoring and fraud detection. The financial world has never been more digitized, and that means the risk of identity theft has never been higher. But instead of manually checking credit reports and bank statements for suspicious activity, automated fraud detection systems alert users the moment an unusual transaction occurs.

Finally, the wealthiest individuals schedule annual financial check-ups—not because they love analyzing spreadsheets, but because they know that financial conditions change. Tax laws shift, investment allocations require rebalancing, and economic downturns can impact savings strategies. The key to long-term financial stability isn't setting a strategy once—it's reassessing regularly. And by scheduling financial check-ins as recurring calendar events, this too becomes part of an effortless system.

Those who automate wealth protection don't wake up one day to discover they've been overpaying for insurance, that they're the victim of fraud, or that they've lost money due to mismanaged assets. Instead, they prevent these problems from occurring in the first place.

For decades, people believed that financial success was about hard work, budgeting, and self-control. But that belief is a relic of a time when people had no choice but to manually manage money. The truth is, in today's world, technology removes the need for discipline.

Instead of forcing yourself to save, automate savings. Instead of manually picking investments, use AI-driven platforms to build a portfolio for you. Instead of constantly monitoring spending, set up alerts that warn you before financial drift happens.

The people who thrive financially in the coming decades will not be the ones who obsess over their finances every day. They will be the ones who set up intelligent systems that make financial success inevitable.

The only question is: Are you using technology to your advantage, or are financial inefficiencies quietly eating away at your wealth? The next step is simple—choose one area of your finances today and integrate technology to optimize it. Whether it's automating savings, using a robo-advisor, or setting up a smarter tax plan, the key is to start now.

The financial winners of the future won't be those who work the hardest at managing money—they will be those who use financial technology to do the work for them.

PASSING WEALTH AND
FINANCIAL WISDOM
TO FUTURE
GENERATIONS

Chapter 17 - How to Stop the Government from Taking Half Your Wealth

Mark had spent his entire adult life building something from nothing. He was the son of immigrants, arriving in Toronto with nothing but the promise of hard work. By the time he reached his fifties, his construction business was thriving, his portfolio had grown, and he was looking forward to an early retirement where he could finally enjoy the fruits of his labor. But in 2004, an unexpected heart attack cut his life short, and with it, the certainty of what would happen to everything he had worked for.

Like many successful entrepreneurs, Mark had always assumed that his wealth would simply pass to his family. He had no will, no trust, no designated executor—only an assumption that his wife and children would sort things out amongst themselves. What followed instead was three years of legal battles. Without a clear estate plan, his business partners contested ownership of the company, creditors came forward with claims, and taxes devoured nearly half of the wealth he had accumulated. By the time his children finally received their inheritance, what should have been a multi-million-dollar legacy had been reduced to a fraction of what it once was.

Mark's story is not unique. The failure to plan an estate is one of the most common and costly financial mistakes that people make—not just among the ultra-wealthy, but among middle-class professionals, entrepreneurs, and anyone with assets that matter. Seventy percent of wealth transfers fail by the second generation. Not because of reckless spending or bad investments, but because of a failure to establish a clear roadmap for how wealth should be passed down. Estate planning isn't just about protecting wealth—it's about controlling what happens to it when you are no longer around to make those decisions yourself.

Estate Planning is Not Just for the Wealthy—It's for the Prepared

One of the biggest myths in personal finance is that estate planning is only necessary if you have millions of dollars in assets. The reality is, if you own anything of value, you have an estate. It doesn't matter whether you own a condo in Vancouver, a stock portfolio in a TFSA, or a growing retirement fund. If you do not have a plan in place, someone else—whether it's the courts, tax agencies, or family members caught in a legal battle—will decide what happens to your assets.

Consider a young professional in his early thirties. He has a $200,000 investment portfolio, a $600,000 condo, and $30,000 in savings. On paper, he may not consider himself "wealthy," but by definition, he has a million-dollar estate. If something were to happen to him tomorrow, what would happen to that money? Would it automatically go to his family? Would it be tied up in probate court for years? Would the government claim a portion of it through unnecessary taxes? The answer to all of those questions depends entirely on whether he has an estate plan.

Estate planning is not about the size of your assets; it's about control. With a plan, you decide who gets what, how much they receive, and when they receive it. Without a plan, the government steps in, and suddenly, the wealth you worked for becomes a legal and financial mess.

For young professionals, the assumption is often that estate planning is something to think about later in life. But the earlier you start, the more protected your assets will be as they grow. More importantly, estate planning isn't just about what happens after death—it's also about what happens if you become incapacitated.

Imagine suffering a medical emergency that leaves you unable to make decisions for yourself. Who would be able to access your bank accounts to pay your bills? Who would handle your investments? Who would make medical decisions on your behalf? Without a legal power of attorney in place, these questions would be decided by the courts, not by you.

For generations, people have been told that writing a will is the cornerstone of estate planning. It's often treated as a checklist item—something to be done later in life, after accumulating wealth or starting a family. But this is where most people go wrong. A will is not a plan. It's a document. And a document, no matter how thorough, does not ensure that wealth moves efficiently across generations, avoids legal entanglements, or minimizes tax liabilities. This is why the wealthy don't just rely on wills—they structure their estates using a combination of trusts, tax strategies, and asset protections that make the transition seamless.

The real difference between families who preserve their wealth and those who lose it within a generation is not income level, financial luck, or even investment choices. It's structure—how assets are arranged, how ownership is defined, and how the inevitable transfer of wealth is managed long before it becomes a crisis. The wealthy do not wait until they are old to think about estate planning, nor do they assume that a basic will is enough. They build a financial architecture that ensures their money serves their families—not the courts, not the tax authorities, and not the legal system.

Wills vs. Trusts—Why Most People Get This Wrong

The first and most persistent mistake people make when thinking about estate planning is assuming that a will is the ultimate tool for passing down wealth. While wills are certainly necessary, they come with a serious limitation: they do not bypass probate. Probate is the long, often expensive process where the court determines the validity of the will, settles outstanding debts, and ensures that assets are distributed as intended. Even the most well-drafted will cannot escape this legal process, which means your heirs could be left waiting months or even years before receiving their inheritance.

This is why the wealthy do not rely solely on wills—they use trusts to bypass probate and dictate the exact terms of how their wealth is distributed. A trust is not just a legal document but a living financial strategy. Unlike a will, which only takes effect upon death, a trust is active while you are alive, meaning that assets can be transferred, managed, and protected without waiting for courts to approve anything.

Different types of trusts serve different strategic purposes:

- **Revocable Living Trusts** allow the owner to maintain control over their assets while ensuring a seamless transition upon death. Because the assets in the trust are not technically owned by the deceased at the time of passing, they do not go through probate. Instead, they transfer **directly to beneficiaries**—saving months, if not years, of legal processing time.

- **Testamentary Trusts** are ideal for parents who want to leave wealth to minor children but do not want those children to receive a lump sum upon turning 18. These trusts allow controlled distributions, ensuring that an inheritance lasts and is used responsibly.
- **Spousal Trusts** protect assets for a surviving spouse while also ensuring that those assets do not become entangled in potential future marriages or creditor claims. This is especially useful for high-net-worth individuals who want to provide financial security for their spouse but also ensure that children from a previous marriage inherit what was originally intended for them.

The key takeaway is simple: a will tells people what you wanted. A trust ensures it happens automatically—without government interference, probate court delays, or financial loss.

The Probate Trap—How to Avoid It

For those unfamiliar with probate, it seems like a straightforward process—an estate goes through court, assets are distributed, and beneficiaries receive their inheritance. But anyone who has actually experienced probate firsthand knows that it is an unnecessarily slow, expensive, and often unpredictable legal process.

In Canada, probate can take six months to two years, depending on the complexity of the estate. In the U.S., the process can last even longer if disputes arise. And while probate fees vary by province or state, they can range anywhere from 1% to 5% of the estate's total value—a massive expense, especially for wealth that could have otherwise transferred directly to beneficiaries.

The wealthy do not tolerate these inefficiencies. They ensure that their assets never touch probate court, using a combination of simple but powerful strategies:

- **Joint Ownership with Right of Survivorship:** This ensures that assets, such as real estate and joint bank accounts, transfer **immediately** to the surviving owner upon death. Since ownership is already shared, the courts do not need to get involved.
- **Beneficiary Designations on Financial Accounts:** Many registered accounts—such as **RRSPs and TFSAs in Canada, or 401(k)s and IRAs in the U.S.**—allow account holders to name beneficiaries. By doing so, these assets **bypass probate entirely** and are transferred directly to the named individuals.
- **Using Trusts to Control Asset Distribution:** As mentioned earlier, **placing assets into a trust ensures they do not go through probate.** Whether it's real estate, stock portfolios, or business assets, trusts allow for seamless and controlled wealth transfers.

To illustrate how crucial these strategies are, consider two scenarios:

Scenario 1: The Traditional Will Approach

Emma, a single mother in British Columbia, has a $1 million estate consisting of a home, savings, and investments. She has a will, but no trust. When she passes away, her assets go through probate. Her children wait nearly two years before receiving their inheritance, and $40,000 in probate fees is deducted from her estate. Meanwhile, legal battles arise over certain assets, delaying the process further.

Scenario 2: The Structured Estate Plan

Michael, also from British Columbia, has a similar $1 million estate. But he structured his estate plan differently. His home is owned jointly with his spouse, ensuring an immediate transfer upon death. His investment accounts have named beneficiaries, avoiding probate. His remaining assets are placed in a revocable living trust, which ensures that his children receive their inheritance within weeks, rather than years. His total probate fees? Zero.

The difference between these two outcomes is not wealth level—but structure.

The RRSP/401(k) Tax Trap—And How to Avoid It

For Canadians and Americans alike, registered retirement accounts—RRSPs in Canada and 401(k)s in the U.S.—are considered essential tools for building wealth. These accounts offer tax-deferred growth, meaning that money grows without being taxed until withdrawal. The appeal is simple: by contributing to these accounts, people can reduce their taxable income during their working years, effectively paying less tax in the present while building a nest egg for the future.

But what happens when that money is passed down? Most people assume that their heirs will simply inherit their RRSP or 401(k) tax-free. The reality is far more costly.

When an RRSP or 401(k) is passed to a non-spouse beneficiary—such as a child or grandchild—the government considers it fully taxable income in the year of death. This means that if someone has a $500,000 RRSP at the time of their passing, nearly half of it could be lost to taxes, depending on their province or state's marginal tax rates. The same account that was carefully built over a lifetime could be gutted in an instant simply due to a lack of planning.

The question, then, is how to minimize the damage. The wealthy use several tactics to reduce this tax burden:

1. **Spousal Rollovers:** In Canada and the U.S., RRSPs and 401(k)s can be transferred **tax-free** to a surviving spouse. This allows the assets to continue growing tax-deferred rather than being hit with an immediate tax bill. But this is only a temporary solution—it does not eliminate taxation, only delays it until the spouse also passes.

2. **Converting RRSPs to RRIFs (Registered Retirement Income Funds):** Instead of keeping RRSPs intact, many financial advisors recommend gradually converting them into RRIFs, which allows for smaller, controlled withdrawals over time. By doing this, retirees can smooth out their taxable income, reducing the risk of a massive tax hit all at once when passing the account to heirs.

3. **Strategic Charitable Giving:** Another overlooked strategy is using charitable donations to offset taxes. If someone with a large RRSP plans ahead, they can leave a portion of their estate to a charity, which in turn generates a tax credit that reduces the overall estate tax burden. This not only allows for a portion of wealth to go to meaningful causes but also ensures that the remainder of the estate faces lower tax liabilities.

The key insight here is simple: RRSPs and 401(k)s are powerful tools for building wealth, but when passed down incorrectly, they can become one of the most expensive assets to inherit.

Using Life Insurance as a Tax Shield

When most people think of life insurance, they see it as a safety net—a way to provide financial support for loved ones in the event of an untimely death. But what they don't realize is that life insurance is also one of the most powerful tax-free wealth transfer tools available.

For high-net-worth individuals, life insurance is not just about protection—it is a strategic tax shelter. Unlike RRSPs or 401(k)s, which are taxable upon death, a properly structured life insurance policy pays out tax-free. This means that a $1 million life insurance payout goes directly to beneficiaries without probate, without estate taxes, and without delay.

This is why the wealthy often use permanent life insurance policies—such as Whole Life or Universal Life insurance—not for income replacement, but for estate planning. These policies serve as a tax-efficient way to pass down wealth, ensuring that assets lost to taxation can be replaced by a tax-free insurance payout.

Consider a high-earning professional who has built an investment portfolio worth $2 million. Without tax planning, their estate could face a 40% tax bill, meaning $800,000 could be lost to taxes before their children ever see a dollar. But if they strategically purchase a $1 million life insurance policy, their heirs effectively receive a tax-free buffer that offsets the losses—preserving the family's financial legacy.

Life insurance, then, is not just a policy. It is a financial tool designed to protect wealth from the government.

Strategic Gifting Before Death

The simplest way to avoid taxes on an estate is also the most obvious: reduce the size of the taxable estate while still alive. In Canada, there is no inheritance tax, but capital gains tax applies when assets are transferred at death. This means that if an individual owns a rental property, a stock portfolio, or other appreciating assets, their heirs could face a hefty tax bill.

One way to minimize this is through gifting assets strategically before death. By gradually transferring ownership of assets over time, rather than all at once upon death, individuals can spread out the tax burden and ensure that more wealth is transferred tax-efficiently.

In the U.S., a similar strategy exists through annual gift exclusions. The IRS allows individuals to gift up to $18,000 per person per year (as of 2024) without incurring gift taxes. By systematically gifting assets over several years, wealth can be transferred without triggering estate taxes, keeping more money within the family. This approach is particularly effective for business owners, real estate investors, and those with large taxable accounts. Instead of waiting until death to pass on wealth, strategic gifting ensures that assets are gradually moved into the hands of heirs while the original owner is still alive—reducing the estate's overall tax burden.

Most people assume that estate planning is about death. But in reality, it's about life—the life of your wealth, the security of your family, and the ability to control what happens even when you're not here. Those who plan their estates correctly are not just protecting their money—they are protecting their loved ones from financial uncertainty and unnecessary legal battles.

The question is simple: Do you want to leave your wealth to your family, or to the courts and tax authorities?

The choice is yours.

The next step is to schedule a financial check-up and begin structuring an estate plan today. Whether it's setting up a will, exploring trusts, or simply naming beneficiaries, the actions you take now will determine whether your financial legacy endures—or disappears.

Conclusion

In 2010, a young couple in Vancouver inherited a windfall—$500,000 from an unexpected family estate settlement. They had been struggling with student loans and were barely keeping up with their mortgage payments. Suddenly, they found themselves with more money than they had ever imagined having in their bank account. It felt like they had won the financial lottery.

At first, they made what seemed like responsible choices. They paid off their loans, upgraded to a slightly bigger home, and finally took the vacation they had put off for years. But they also made a series of subtle, seemingly harmless decisions: they bought a new car because they "deserved it," dined out more frequently because they could "afford it," and slowly let go of the cautious spending habits that had defined their life before the inheritance.

Five years later, they were back in debt. The windfall had evaporated, not because of a single reckless decision but because they had never learned how to manage money in the first place. The sudden influx of wealth had only magnified their existing financial habits—some good, many bad.

Their story is not unique. Research shows that 70% of lottery winners go broke within a few years and that wealthy families tend to lose their fortunes by the third generation. The real challenge in personal finance isn't about making money—it's about keeping it, growing it, and protecting it over time.

And that is where we arrive at the most important lesson of this book: your financial success is not about how much you earn, but about how well you manage what you have.

Over the course of this book, we've dismantled some of the most pervasive myths about money. We've challenged the idea that budgeting is the ultimate solution, exposed why many people get trapped in cycles of debt, and explored how investing is not just for the wealthy, but for anyone who understands its fundamental principles.

You've learned how to create a financial roadmap that aligns with your life goals. Not just a vague wish list, but an actual strategy—one that allows you to prioritize what matters most, build financial security, and leverage wealth-building strategies that work even when you're sleeping.

You've discovered that saving money isn't about restriction—it's about designing a system that makes saving effortless. We explored how automation removes human error, why psychology matters more than math in financial decisions, and how small, consistent changes lead to exponential financial growth over time.

You've also faced the reality of debt—not as an enemy to be feared, but as a tool that, when used wisely, can create financial leverage. We dissected the difference between good debt and bad debt, examined how credit scores shape financial opportunities, and uncovered why interest rates are one of the most critical factors in long-term wealth building.

We dove deep into the world of investing, stripping away the complexity that often intimidates first-time investors. You now understand that investing isn't about chasing the next hot stock or timing the market—it's about playing the long game, embracing diversification, and letting compound interest do the heavy lifting.

And we talked about the often-overlooked yet essential aspect of financial health: protection. From estate planning to insurance, from tax efficiency to economic downturns, you've learned that wealth is not just about what you build, but what you safeguard against loss.

Knowledge without action is useless.

You can understand every financial principle in this book, but if you don't take deliberate action, nothing will change. The difference between those who struggle financially and those who achieve financial independence isn't intelligence, luck, or even income—it's consistent execution.

So, where do you go from here?

- **Revisit your financial goals.** What do you actually want your money to do for you? Define clear, measurable objectives that go beyond "I want to be rich."
- **Automate your financial systems.** If you haven't set up automated savings, debt payments, or investments yet, do it today. One small decision can transform your financial future.
- **Start investing—even if it's a small amount.** The biggest mistake people make is waiting until they feel "ready." The market rewards time, not timing.
- **Eliminate financial waste.** Go through your last three months of expenses and identify what you're spending money on that doesn't serve your goals. Redirect that money toward your financial priorities.

- **Increase your financial resilience.** Build an emergency fund, reduce unnecessary risk, and ensure your financial future is protected against unforeseen events.

Every financial journey is unique, but the principles remain universal. The strategies in this book are designed to be timeless, adaptable, and effective whether you're just starting out or looking to refine an existing financial plan.

Imagine your life five years from now.

What if you had no financial anxiety—no sleepless nights worrying about debt, no fear of unexpected expenses, no panic at the thought of retirement? What if you had enough savings to take the risks you've always wanted to take—starting your own business, taking time off to travel, or switching careers without financial stress?

What if you could look back and say, "I made the right decisions when it mattered most"?

That's the future this book is helping you build.

Financial freedom isn't just about being rich—it's about having choices. It's about being able to say "yes" to the things that matter and "no" to the things that don't. It's about knowing that no matter what happens, you have the knowledge and systems in place to weather financial storms and come out stronger.

But achieving this future requires one thing: commitment.

As you move forward, remember these guiding principles:

- **Financial success is a system, not a one-time event.** It's about setting up repeatable habits that compound over time.
- **Your income is not your wealth.** True wealth comes from financial security, not just a high salary.
- **You don't need to be perfect—you just need to be consistent.** Progress, not perfection, is what leads to lasting financial transformation.
- **Financial literacy is an ongoing journey.** Keep learning, keep adapting, and never assume you know everything.

Most importantly, **your financial future is in your hands.**

No one is coming to fix your finances for you. Not your employer, not the government, not a financial guru. The responsibility—and the power—rests with you.

So, as you close this book, ask yourself:

- What is the **first financial action** I will take today?
- What is the **long-term goal** I will commit to achieving?
- How will I hold myself accountable for building the financial future I deserve?

Your money. Your choices. Your future.

Make it count.

Your financial future isn't something you 'get around to'—it's something you take charge of today. Wealth isn't built overnight, but every decision you make—starting right now—moves you one step closer.

The difference between financial security and financial struggle isn't intelligence or luck—it's action. So take the first step. Automate your savings. Invest even a small amount. Cut wasteful spending. And most importantly, commit to financial literacy for the long haul.

Because your money should work for you—not the other way around.

Appendix: Jargon Buster

A simple guide to understanding complex financial terms used in this book.

General Finance Terms (A-C)

1. **Amortization** – Gradually paying off a loan over time through regular payments.
2. **Annual Percentage Rate (APR)** – The total yearly cost of borrowing money, including interest and fees.
3. **Appreciation** – When the value of an asset (like a house or stock) goes up over time.
4. **Arbitrage** – Buying something in one market and selling it in another to make a profit.
5. **Asset** – Anything valuable you own, like cash, real estate, or stocks.
6. **Asset Allocation** – Dividing investments among different categories to manage risk.
7. **Bankruptcy** – A legal process when someone can't pay their debts and seeks protection from creditors.

8. **Bear Market** – A prolonged period when stock prices fall by at least 20%.
9. **Benchmark** – A standard used to measure an investment's performance (e.g., S&P 500 for stocks).
10. **Bond** – A loan investors give to companies or governments in exchange for interest payments.
11. **Book Value** – The value of an asset according to accounting records, not necessarily its market price.
12. **Broker** – A person or company that buys and sells investments on your behalf.
13. **Bull Market** – A period when stock prices keep going up over time.
14. **Capital Gains** – The profit you make when selling an investment for more than you paid.
15. **Capital Gains Tax** – The tax you pay on profits from selling investments.
16. **Cash Flow** – The movement of money in and out of your account over time.
17. **Collateral** – Something valuable (like a house or car) pledged to a lender to secure a loan.
18. **Compounding** – When earnings (interest or dividends) generate additional earnings over time.
19. **Consumer Price Index (CPI)** – A measure of inflation tracking the cost of everyday goods.

20. **Cryptocurrency** – Digital money like Bitcoin that isn't controlled by a government or bank.
21. **Current Ratio** – A measure of a company's ability to pay short-term liabilities with short-term assets.
22. **Callable Bond** – A bond that an issuer can repay before its maturity date

Real Estate Terms

23. **Adjustable-Rate Mortgage (ARM)** – A home loan with an interest rate that changes over time.
24. **Amortization Period** – The total time it takes to pay off a mortgage.
25. **Appraisal** – An expert's estimate of how much a property is worth.
26. **Bridge Loan** – A short-term loan used until long-term financing is available.
27. **Capital Gains Tax (Real Estate)** – Tax on the profit from selling a property that isn't your principal residence.
28. **Closing Costs** – Extra fees (legal fees, taxes, etc.) paid when buying or selling a home.
29. **Condominium (Condo)** – A type of property where you own your unit but share common areas with others.

30. **Down Payment** – The upfront money you pay when buying a home (usually 5-20% of the price).
31. **Equity in Real Estate** – The portion of your home you own outright (home value minus mortgage balance).
32. **Escrow** – A neutral third party that holds money or property until conditions are met.
33. **Fixed-Rate Mortgage** – A home loan with the same interest rate for the entire term.
34. **Foreclosure** – When a lender takes back a property because the owner failed to make mortgage payments.
35. **Home Equity Line of Credit (HELOC)** – A loan that lets you borrow money using your home as collateral.
36. **Mortgage Pre-Approval** – When a lender tells you how much they'll let you borrow before you buy a house.
37. **Mortgage Refinancing** – Replacing your current mortgage with a new one to get better terms.
38. **Principal Residence Exemption (PRE)** – A tax rule that lets you sell your home without paying capital gains tax.
39. **Real Estate Investment Trust (REIT)** – A company that owns income-producing properties, like malls or apartments, and lets investors buy shares.
40. **Zoning Laws** – Local rules about how land can be used (residential, commercial, industrial, etc.).

Insurance Terms

41. **Actuary** – A professional who calculates risk for insurance companies.
42. **Beneficiary** – The person who receives money from an insurance policy when the insured person dies.
43. **Claim** – A request for payment from an insurance company after an accident or loss.
44. **Comprehensive Coverage** – A type of auto insurance that covers damage from theft, natural disasters, or vandalism.
45. **Deductible** – The amount you must pay out of pocket before your insurance covers the rest.
46. **Disability Insurance** – Pays you money if you can't work due to illness or injury.
47. **Exclusions** – Situations or conditions that an insurance policy does not cover.
48. **Health Savings Account (HSA)** – A tax-advantaged account for medical expenses in the U.S.
49. **Life Insurance** – A policy that pays money to your beneficiaries when you die.
50. **Liability Insurance** – Covers damages or injuries you cause to others (common in auto and home insurance).
51. **Underinsured Motorist Coverage** – Insurance that helps if you're hit by someone without enough coverage.

Tax Terms

52. **Adjusted Gross Income (AGI)** – Your total income minus certain deductions, used to calculate taxes.
53. **Capital Gains Tax** – A tax on profits from selling investments, real estate, or other assets.
54. **Charitable Tax Deduction** – A tax break for donations made to registered charities.
55. **Corporate Tax** – Taxes paid by businesses on their profits.
56. **Deduction** – Expenses that lower your taxable income, like mortgage interest or student loan interest.
57. **Deferred Tax** – Taxes that you owe but can be paid later, like in RRSPs or 401(k)s.
58. **Tax Shelter** – A legal strategy to reduce taxable income.
59. **Withholding Tax** – The amount of money an employer withholds from an employee's paycheck for taxes.

Made in the USA
Monee, IL
04 November 2026

67381898R00164